Jack Hibberd
Selected Plays:

White With Wire Wheels
Dimboola
Stretch of the Imagination

CURRENCY PRESS
The performing arts publisher

CURRENCY PLAYS
General Editor: Katharine Brisbane

First published 2000
Currency Press Ltd,
Gadigal Land, Suite 310, 46–56 Kippax Street, Surry Hills, NSW 2010, Australia
enquiries@currency.com.au
www.currency.com.au

Reprinted 2014, 2015, 2016, 2020, 2024.

White With Wire Wheels was first published in *Four Australian Plays* by Penguin Books, Harmondsworth, Middlesex, and Ringwood, Victoria, 1970; *A Stretch of the Imagination* by Currency Press, 1972; and *Dimboola*, with *The Last of the Knucklemen* by John Powers, by Penguin Books, Harmondsworth, Middlesex, and Ringwood, Victoria, 1974.

Introduction © Paul McGillick, 2000; *White With Wire Wheels* © Jack Hibberd, 1967; *A Stretch of the Imagination* © Jack Hibberd, 1972; *Dimboola* © Jack Hibberd, Lorraine Milne, 1969, 1973.

COPYING FOR EDUCATIONAL PURPOSES
The Australian *Copyright Act 1968* (Act) allows a maximum of one chapter or 10% of this book, whichever is the greater, to be copied by any educational institution for its educational purposes provided that that educational institution (or the body that administers it) has given a remuneration notice to Copyright Agency Limited (CAL) under the Act.

For details of the CAL licence for educational institutions contact CAL, 19/157 Liverpool Street, Sydney, NSW, 2000. Tel: (02) 9394 7600; Fax: (02) 9394 7601; E-mail: info@copyright.com.au

COPYING FOR OTHER PURPOSES
Except as permitted under the Act, for example a fair dealing for the purposes of study, research, criticism or review, no part of this book may be reproduced, stored in a retrieval system, or transmitted in any form or by any means without prior written permission. All inquiries should be made to the publisher at the address above.

Any performance or public reading of *White With Wire Wheels*, *A Stretch of the Imagination* or *Dimboola* is forbidden unless a licence has been received from the author or the author's agent. The purchase of this book in no way gives the purchaser the right to perform the play in public, whether by means of a staged production or a reading. All applications for public performance should be made in advance and directed to Bryson Agency Australia Pty. Ltd., P.O. Box 226 Flinders Lane P.O., Melbourne, 8009, Victoria, Australia; phone: 613.9620.9100; fax: 613.9621.2788; email: agency@bryson.com.au.

In accordance with the requirement of the Australian Media, Entertainment & Arts Alliance, Currency Press has made every effort to identify, and gain permission of, the artists who appear in the photographs which illustrate these plays.

NATIONAL LIBRARY OF AUSTRALIA CIP DATA
   Hibberd, Jack, 1940–.
   [Selections]
   Selected plays.
   ISBN 0 86819 632 0.
   I. Title.
   A822.3

Set by Dean Nottle.
Cover design by Kate Florance.
Cover picture: Max Gillies as Monk O'Neill in the 1976 Australian Performing Group, Melbourne, production of *A Stretch of the Imagination*. (Photo: Brendan Hennessy)

Currency Press acknowledges the Traditional Owners of the Country on which we live and work. We pay our respects to all Aboriginal and Torres Strait Islander Elders, past and present.

JACK HIBBERD was born in the Victorian regional city of Bendigo in 1940. His first play, *White With Wire Wheels*, premiered at the University of Melbourne in 1967, and was followed in the same year by *Three Old Friends*, the first play to be produced at Carlton's La Mama Theatre.

The next decade or so saw many of his plays produced by the group of theatre workers based in Carlton at both La Mama and the Australian Performing Group's Pram Factory. These included *Dimboola* (1969), *Marvellous Melbourne* (co-written with John Romeril, 1970), *A Stretch of the Imagination* (1972), *Captain Midnight VC* (1972), *Peggy Sue* (1974), *The Les Darcy Show* (1974), *A Toast To Melba* (1976) and *A Man of Many Parts* (1979, later reworked in the 90s as *A History of the Western World in Ninety Minutes*).

Other plays followed in the 1980s, including a large cycle of plays, *Musical Parts: Mothballs* (1980), *Lavender Bags* (1981), *Glycerine Tears* (1982), *The Old School Tie* and *Malarky Barks* (1983); a short play collection, *Squibs* (1984); and an adaptation of Guy de Maupassant's *Odyssey of a Prostitute* for the Adelaide Festival.

From the mid-80s he left off writing for the stage and resumed medical practice. However, he continued to write novels, non-fiction, poetry, short stories and screenplays.

His return to stage writing in 1993 has resulted in numerous plays since, including *Female Rhapsodies, Slam Dunk, Blood Bath, Repossession, Bedlam Ballads* and a dramatic adaptation of Tolstoy's *The Death of Ivan Ilych*. In all, he has written nearly 40 plays to date.

Hibberd died in 2024.

Contents

vii   INTRODUCTION
Paul McGillick

1   WHITE WITH WIRE WHEELS

65   DIMBOOLA

107   A STRETCH OF THE IMAGINATION

PICTURE SOURCES

White with Wire Wheels: page 8, Mitchell Library, State Library of NSW; page 59, from the author's collection.

Dimboola: pages 87, 88 and 108 (top), courtesy of the *Age*; page 108 (bottom), Coralie Wood and Partners; page 107, courtesy Michael Leunig

A Stretch of the Imagination: pages 122, 130, 132, and 143, from the Currency Press collection.

Introduction

Paul McGillick

Many people still think of Jack Hibberd exclusively in terms of his association with the Melbourne theatrical *avant-garde* of the late 1960s and 70s which rebelled against a diet of English and American plays to create a new theatre using an Australian voice and set in an Australian context.

A number of things need to be said about this—both about Hibberd himself and the Melbourne theatre scene at the time. It is necessary because, with the passage of time and our unavoidable dependence on oral history (no comprehensive account of that period has yet been published), a powerful mythologising process is under way. Inevitably, this brings with it all kinds of falsifications as a new generation seeks to make itself independent of the past. Much is either forgotten, misremembered or misrepresented.

But to lose the links to our artistic past is also to lose the foundation for future practice. Cultural amnesia can have a destructive effect on the individuals who are casually thrown out with what is seen as historical garbage. This is not just unfair, but also culturally wasteful. Hibberd has suffered a lot from this kind of ignorance. So much so, that many are unaware that he continues to write for the theatre (and his work continues to evolve), he has published a number of novels and poetry collections, not to mention an important medical textbook.

But equally, such amnesia condemns future generations endlessly to re-invent the wheel. As with Prometheus, the mythological embodiment of the creative will, our cultural liver grows each day only to be torn out again the next.

Firstly, to deal with the theatrical *avant-garde* of the time, it needs to be pointed out that they not only had the 'Australianising' agenda I have already mentioned, but that this was part of a broader agenda. Importantly, they were concerned with investigating the nature of the theatre as a whole and they hungrily took whatever was on offer—radical theatre in the United States, the experiments of Peter Brook and the Royal Shakespeare Company in Britain, Jerzy Grotowski in Poland and writer/directors like Eugenio Barba and Richard Schechner who were investigating the anthropology of the theatre all over the world.

This resulted in extensive experimentation with actor training, *mise-en-scène* and script-writing. It also involved re-thinking the role of the audience and the way audiences and performers should relate to one another in the performing space. One result was the abandonment of a fixed space (in particular, the proscenium arch stage) and the adoption of a flexible approach, so that a unique actor-audience relationship evolved for each individual production.

This implied political and social agendas. It was the time of the Vietnam War and the increasing dissent against that military adventure inevitably brought with it a general questioning of social and political values in Australia. The *avant-garde* involved itself in the social and political idealism of the time and the content of its work reflected this—as did the experiments with agit-prop theatre and street theatre (which was invariably political). It is crucial, however, to understand that the theatre itself became a metaphor for this exploration into how we could create a new and better society.

The actor-audience relationship was part of this metaphor. So too was the cultivation of a new audience altogether—of people who never previously went to the theatre. Australian football became an important bridge here. It was seen as a form of theatrical populism from which the orthodox theatre could learn. Football became a subject (Barry Oakley and David Williamson both wrote plays using football as a subject, and football images litter the work of writers like Hibberd, Garrie Hutchinson and Barry Dickins). Football even became the occasion of extended political agitation when the Australian Performing Group (APG) supported the players strike at the Essendon Football Club in the late 1960s and Carlton player, Brent Crosswell, when he was victimised for having long hair and supposedly smoking marijuana on game days.

Hibberd, as a key writer right from the beginning, was a part of this milieu. While he shared the spirit of social and political revival, he did not necessarily share the increasingly strident left-wing proclivities of the APG. Moreover, he (and others like actor/director, Graeme Blundell) felt increasingly uncomfortable with the less-than-rational ideologising which insisted on a highly collectivist approach to theatre-making which robbed directors and writers of their autonomy.

What had happened was that Hibberd had retained his interest in exploring the nature and origins of the modern theatre while the APG as a whole had become preoccupied with ideological posturing and a vague notion of theatre-as-lifestyle—which in this case involved communal living and drug-taking.

This brings us to a very important issue as we address these three classic, early Hibberd plays.

Certainly, Hibberd was from the beginning concerned with using the language of his audience, and his work continues to mine the riches of Australian English in the quest for an authentic and creative voice. Similarly, he has always used Australia as the social context of his plays—although he has ranged beyond Australia in some later plays such as *The Overcoat* (1976) and *Odyssey of a Prostitute* (1984), while most of the monodramas could be set anywhere.

However, Hibberd has always seen himself as a modernist, a position he reinforced in an article for *The Australian's Review of Books* (December, 1999) where he spoke in passing of the APG's limited interest in the same issue:

> In truth, the APG only partly grappled with some of modernism's sinewy innovations, and were significant, memorable, for the creation of a uniquely expressive Australian physical and comic style, which was native and only slantingly related to modernism. The two must not be confused.

Modernism is a problematic term because no one completely agrees with anyone else as to what it actually means. Its character, however, can be summed up as being critical, universalist and idealistic.

It is critical because it takes as its starting point the idea that reality is relative and depends on individual and cultural points of view. Accordingly, modernist art aims to question taken-for-granted notions of reality, including the tradition of art itself. Crucially, it argues that all art grows out of a tradition, but that the tradition needs to be constantly interrogated if it is not to become sterile convention. One of the originators of modernism, T.S. Eliot, comments in 'Tradition and the Individual Talent':

> What happens when a new work of art is created is something that happens simultaneously to all the works of art which preceded it. The existing monuments form an ideal order among themselves, which is modified by the introduction of the new (the really new) work of art among them. The existing order is complete before the new work arrives; for order to persist after the supervention of novelty, the whole existing order must be, if ever so slightly, altered.

Modernism is universalist in that it aims to develop forms which communicate directly to its audience without the need for translation. Hence, we have Eliot's notion of the objective correlative, modernist architecture's rejection of ornament and the bias towards abstraction in the visual arts.

Implicit in this second characteristic is the third—the social and political idealism of modernism. Le Corbusier's free plan was deeply radical because it effectively argued for the endless re-cycling of buildings instead of the fundamentally consumerist notion of functionally specific buildings. Likewise, modernist theatre called into question social hierarchies, not only by questioning theatrical convention, but also by emphasising the role of the audience in generating the meaning of the performance.

This might be called an existentialist position because the meaning of the work is not prescribed, but has to be generated by an interaction between the artist and the audience through the medium of the artwork.

These three principles inform Jack Hibberd's approach to the theatre and have done so from the start, even in these three early and apparently very 'Australian' plays.

He is preoccupied with writing plays which grow out of the Western tradition of theatre, but which at the same time vigorously and creatively question that tradition. His theatrical objective is to engender critical reflection on the part of his audience. But he vehemently eschews what he describes as 'social studies theatre', a brand of naturalism which he feels has hijacked the Australian theatre and which uses the theatre only in order to *illustrate* social and political agendas. Instead, Hibberd aims to generate theatrical metaphors and a theatre which speaks directly to its audience in its own language without need for intermediary translation.

As we know, modernism had from its inception the seeds of a certain authoritarianism which tended to impose the wrong sort of universalism— namely making everything look and sound the same. One reaction against this was a revived regionalism, a celebration of the vernacular. Once again, this is something Hibberd holds in contempt as something shallow, contrived and sentimental, its local setting, topical themes and self-conscious use of Australian English masking a fundamental artistic failure.

A useful term to describe Hibberd, I think, is one popularised by the architectural critic, Kenneth Frampton. He talks about *critical regionalism* to describe a kind of architecture which is of its own place, but which reinterprets that specific character within the framework of a universal tradition and of modernity. As Hibberd remarks in his *Review of Books* article: 'I am urging the incorporation of vital ingredients of the past, not replicating literally the past.'

In fact, Hibberd condemns the contemporary theatre in Australia as being ignorant of the tradition from which it ostensibly springs:

> … events, individuals and organisations have conspired to deny Australian audiences the rich fruits of twentieth century theatrical Modernism, the greatest epoch of stage inventiveness since the English and Spanish renaissances, and the most diverse ever in stage history.

Hence, Hibberd's work needs to be understood as growing out of the language, culture and history of Australia. But it does so 'critically'. In other words, the vernacular culture is celebrated, examined and extended through the prism of a greater, more universal cultural tradition. In this way, the particularities of Hibberd's characters and their situations have the potential for universal significance. While he exploits the Australian language, Australian history and mores, he is equally indebted to great modernist playwrights like Brecht, Beckett and Pinter, while the art, music and literature of the modernist tradition are always present, either explicitly or implicitly.

In fact, to look at Hibberd's most recent work—including the re-categorisation of his short plays of the 1980s and 90s as part of a grand musical scheme—we can see that he has effectively come full circle. Having begun with exploring themes and situations which owed a lot to Pinter and Beckett (in his early short plays and *A Stretch of the Imagination*), he has now brought his own focus to a preoccupation he shares with Pinter and Beckett. This is to do with the way form communicates directly with the audience—through the rhythms, harmonies and counterpoint of the dialogue, and through the metaphorical potential of character and situation.

Central to Hibberd's work has always been an anti-naturalistic and anti-illusionist agenda. Even in the early plays, which are his most naturalistic, there are always strategies and gestures which subvert the naturalism. His objective here is engagement: where the illusion of naturalism enables the audience to remain detached from imaginative engagement, anti-naturalism provokes the audience into participation.

The most important way Hibberd does this is by drawing attention to the fact that we are in a theatre, witnessing a theatrical event. Where naturalism aims to distract the audience from the fact that they are in a theatre in order to create the illusion that they are actually somewhere else, Hibberd ironically points up the fact that it is all an illusion.

A little remarked influence on Hibberd has been Shakespeare. It is subtle, but important for the way it has helped Hibberd to develop his key theatrical idea—namely, that the theatre is a metaphor for life and that 'all the world's a stage'. This becomes increasingly explicit, especially in the monodramas (and remembering that *Stretch* is really the first of his monodramas), but is present embryonically in most of the early work, including *White With Wire Wheels*—for example, at the beginning of Scene 8 when Helen makes a very Shakespearean direct address to the audience which refers explicitly to the theatricality of what the audience is witnessing:

> HELEN: The purpose of this play,
> Should the playwright have his way,
> Is general and not particular,
> For Malcolm, Rod and Simon are
> Not simply the blacker side of white.
> Please flip the coin tonight.

The whole act of going to the theatre is for Hibberd a ritual and the theatre itself is a place where the ritual games of life and death are played out. In other words, the theatre is a collective art. Here, we (actors and audience alike) come together in an imaginative reflection on what it means to be human and to participate in the ritualised re-enactment of what Hibberd calls the psychopathology of everyday life.

Rituals are basically of two kinds. One serves to endorse everyday reality and, by repetitive action, confirm that our current beliefs and actions are for the best. The other kind—which also involves the principle of repetition, but only up to a point—is transformative. Such rituals can either serve to propel us to new levels of awareness (for example, rites of passage and healing) or call into question the very beliefs we have so far taken for granted.

Sometimes, the two come together. Hibberd explores this with *Dimboola* (1969) where the wedding reception is both a ritual celebrating the continuity of social life and one which actually creates a new dimension to social reality by bringing together two previously unassociated clans.

Rituals can be both public and private, but both are inherently theatrical because they involve performance. Hibberd explores public ritual most obviously in *Dimboola*. But at the heart of *White With Wire Wheels* are the rituals which bond the three young men—and which provide Hibberd with an early opportunity to explore the paradox of rituals, namely the way in which rituals can be used either to deny reality or to confront it.

The theatre is itself a public ritual and Hibberd, as an essentially comic writer, belongs to a theatrical tradition which not only includes the demotic comedy of Shakespeare, but also the disruptive, iconoclastic, satirical and vulgar spirit of the Rabelaisian carnival, so splendidly described by Mikhail Bakhtin—the established and regular opportunities for the common people to challenge and mock the institutions (church, state and marriage) which normally control their lives. For Hibberd the theatre should be simultaneously comic, poetic and offensive. In so doing, it is just reflecting the reality of human existence.

In *Stretch*, however, Hibberd explores for the first time the *private* rituals which not only give order to our lives, but which provide a means for trying out new personas. Like the rest of us, Monk O'Neill has everyday rituals like eating, urinating and cleaning his teeth. Normally, these would be performed unthinkingly. But Monk, living as a hermit in the outback of Australia, turns these into performances for his own entertainment. More importantly, though, Monk reflects on his life through the imaginative re-enactment of past events. This is a re-creation of his life and an existential statement by the playwright that 'we invent for ourselves the greater part of experience' (Nietzsche).

♦♦♦♦♦

These three plays are classics—if we define a classic by saying that it is a play which has a life long after its first production, therefore lending itself to any number of interpretive approaches. In fact, *Dimboola* is probably the most performed Australian play ever—and not just in Australia, but in many countries around the world where it has been successfully adapted to the local cultural context. It is especially popular with amateur groups which, according to Hibberd, invariably perform it better than professionals. *Stretch* is also regularly revived and it, too, has been successfully staged elsewhere in the world, notably in Shanghai and Beijing in 1987.

But all three plays have an additional importance because, early as they are in Hibberd's career, they map out the thematic and formal issues which have characterised his dramaturgy ever since.

Of the three, *White With Wire Wheels* (Hibberd's first full-length play) seems on the surface to be the most culturally specific and the one most tied to its time. Like much of the work being done at the time at La Mama, it is a satirical challenge to the unquestioned values which seemed (and, frankly, still seem) to underpin Australian society. This is the 'ocker' society, driven by a deep-seated sense of inferiority, philistine, xenophobic, its identity shaped by external forces rather than inner conviction and prone to avoid reality through aggression and alcohol.

Also typical of its time, the play takes the inability of the sexes to relate successfully to one another as the touchstone of a profound social and spiritual malaise.

But Hibberd goes well beyond this localised theme to a more universal application by the way in which he handles his material. He requires, for example, that the three girlfriends and the new arrival, Helen, all be played by the same actress, dressed in the same way. This is a marked symbolic gesture to underline the fact that the three young men effectively see all women as the same. Rather than relate to them as individuals, they view them as interchangeable sexual conveniences and as mother substitutes.

The infantilism of the ocker is highlighted in the pivotal Scene 8 where each of the men pleads to spend the night with Helen in language which is more or less the same for each of them.

> MAL: Just this one night. I won't do anything. I promise. I just want to lie there. I won't bother you ever again.

It is this scene in particular which pushes the play beyond its earlier realism. Firstly, the scene has a highly ritualistic feel to it as each of the young men pay suit to Helen (somewhat reminiscent of *The Merchant of Venice*), each bringing with him a part from a motor car as tribute. Each of the men then has a core speech which reveals deep insecurity and expressed not in naturalistic Australian English, but in a poetically charged language. Each of them is rejected in turn, whereupon each delivers the same soliloquy in verse:

> My head is not exactly clear,
> I don't know what I'm doing,
> My dreams are thick with fear,
> I'm frightened
> And unenlightened,
> I think there's something brewing.

The scene ends with a grotesque tableau of Rod, Mal and Simon huddled together as if in a car travelling at high speed, their car parts forming the shape of a car, in a light which, according to the stage directions, 'should be garish and eerie, e.g. a green'.

INTRODUCTION xv

If the ending of the play suggests Beckett's *Waiting for Godot*
MAL: Let's go!
They stand still. Darkness.
THE END

Scene 8 also reveals another powerful influence on Hibberd's work—the theatre of German Expressionism and playwrights like Frank Wedekind and early Brecht. It also highlights a more universal preoccupation—the image of humanity as lost, lonely and confused, having awoken in a world which is more like a nightmare than a home, a world which is absurd, defying all rational explanation and echoing the lines of A.E. Housman:

I, a stranger and afraid
In a world I never made.

As Hibberd once commented, 'the response of all art… is to see the world as some place which has gone awry'.

Where *White With Wire Wheels* deals in ocker social rituals—driving rapidly and recklessly around the place in motor cars, binge drinking with even sex reduced to a ritual—*Dimboola* takes another ritual, the wedding reception, as the basis for its plot.

The play was written in London in 1969 during Hibberd's first trip away from Australia. Already aware of experiments in audience participation by figures like Grotowski, he had the chance to see a performance by the Living Theatre in London. He was not impressed and felt that such theatre 'subjected theatregoers, even theatre-lovers, to all manner of harassment and contempt—especially from actors with sadistic streaks and those who genuinely despised the paying public'.

Nonetheless, he remained intrigued by the possibility of involving the audience directly in the event, but reached the conclusion that 'any such theatre event must embrace a familiar social ritual, must require the simulation of a ritual in which the audience (the paying public) could readily assume a role'.

There were two precedents for a wedding play—Chekov's short farce, *The Wedding* (1890), and Brecht's one-act farce, *The Bourgeois Wedding* (1919). From the Chekov Hibberd took the notion of a cast of contrasting characters, misunderstandings and misidentifications with a Very Important Person who gives his imprimatur to the occasion. From Brecht he took the mood of uncontrolled absurdity.

Hibberd describes *Dimboola* as a 'balance between satire and celebration'. The ritual is the wedding reception which itself is made up of various ceremonies—toasts, speeches, reading of telegrams, the bridal waltz, etc. In a largely tacit way, everybody at a wedding reception has a prescribed role to play, and everybody gets to be both observer and participant. The play assumes such knowledge on the part of the audience who get to participate, not just passively by sitting, eating and drinking, but also by getting up on the dance floor.

As it turned out, *Dimboola* was the only play Hibberd wrote which involved literal audience participation. It was quickly apparent that any theatre which restricted itself to 'familiar social ritual(s)' would be a very limited theatre. But the seeds of a more sophisticated notion of audience participation were already present in *Dimboola* because Hibberd saw the audience's role in terms of function rather than literal participation. Inevitably this would lead to a metatheatrical role for the audience in which it colludes (in the monodramas, beginning with *Stretch*) with the performer in his/her projection of life as a complex construction of roles, the theatre as a microcosm of the world and the world itself as a metaphorical theatre.

While *Dimboola* is a celebratory parody which derives its efficacy from recognising the inherent theatricality of the wedding reception, it also has a darker side which links it to Hibberd's later work—for example, a cynicism about marriage, relations between the sexes and the illusion of romantic love.

Like the other two plays, *A Stretch of the Imagination* (1972) reveals the modernist preoccupations of the early Hibberd. It is critical in the way it sets up the theatre (through the device of monodrama) as a metaphor for life and then proceeds to challenge our assumptions about it. It is universalist (or critically regionalist, to adopt Frampton's phrase) in the way it takes a culturally specific character, site and language in order to deal with universal themes. And it is idealist in the sense that it implicitly (once again through the device of monodrama) demands that the audience share responsibility with the actor for the meanings which are generated.

Hibberd these days is less sensitive about the 'feral figure of Samuel Beckett' and happily acknowledges the debt *Stretch* owes to *Krapp's Last Tape* and *Waiting for Godot*. The ritualistic circularity of *Stretch* (the play takes place over one day, from dawn to dusk) had already been tested by Hibberd in a short early play, *Just Before the Honeymoon* (1967). The action of the play consists of the rituals with which its sole character, Monk O'Neill, fills each day. It may well be Monk's last day alive. On the other hand, Monk's life is a kind of living death, anyway. In any case, Monk's strict rituals are regularly interrupted by bouts of reflection on the past in which, says Hibberd, he is 'discovering his self through semi-fictive re-creations of his past'.

Monk is a distinctly unpleasant man. But he is also, at the end of the day, a very honest one and there is a strong impression that he has gone into this voluntary exile, living in a humpy on One Tree Hill (he has actually chopped down the tree in a fit of pique), in order to confront his past and through this confrontation to explore his own creativity—in effect, to create himself all over again using the raw materials of the life he has already lived.

Beneath Monk's aggression, crudity and callous rejection of other human beings, there is despair. He has lacked the courage to commit to intimacy (just as Rod, Mal and Simon fear that intimacy might reveal just how emotionally bankrupt they are) and is now on a quest to find his Self. But his quest is paradoxical: he must learn to be alone, but literal aloneness is both solipsistic and narcissistic and can only result in a distorted view of the Self. This is the same narcissism we see in the three young men in *White With White Wheels*, the characteristics of which have been summarised by Christopher Lasch in his book, *The Culture of Narcissism*:

> Dependence on the vicarious warmth provided by others combined with a fear of dependence
> A sense of inner emptiness
> Unsatisfied oral cravings
> Boundless repressed rage
> Avoidance of close involvements which might release intense feelings of rage
> Feelings of hypochondria
> Fantasies of omnipotence and a strong belief in their right to exploit others and be gratified

These are characteristics which Monk shares with the three boys from *White With Wire Wheels*. In fact, one can imagine Rod, Mal or Simon becoming a Monk forty years down the track.

Hibberd's work, then as now, is simultaneously a critique and a comic celebration of Australia. However, his modernist strategies ensure that no matter how comprehensively he draws on the Australian language and context for his raw material, the final product resonates with the universality of human experience that we expect from good art.

As for the comic character—well, the laughs in Hibberd range from the private ironic chuckle to the subversive Rabelaisian belly laugh, from Beckett's 'laugh laughing at the laugh' (the humour of the dark night of the soul) to a raucous appreciation of the contradictions of life. Laughter is both defence and defiance in a world which is incurably mad, irrational and unpredictable. As Monk says at the going down of the sun: 'Not bad for a terminal case'.

Further Reading:

    Hainsworth, John, *Hibberd*. North Ryde: Methuen, 1987
    McGillick, Paul, *Jack Hibberd*. Amsterdam: Rodopi, 1988
    McGillick, Paul, *The Ritual Theatre of Jack Hibberd*. Griffith University, 1997 (Unpub. PhD thesis)

Paul McGillick is a freelance writer on the performing and visual arts, architecture and design.

WHITE WITH WIRE WHEELS

For Jocelyn

White With Wire Wheels was first produced by La Mama Theatre at the University of Melbourne on 26 September 1967 with the following cast:

MAL	Ric Thorpe
ROD	Peter Burleigh
SIMON	Antony Styant-Brown
SUE, CATH, ANNE, HELEN	Sue Ingleton

Produced by David Kendall
Designed by John Funston

CHARACTERS

    MAL, 25 years
    SIMON, 25 years
    ROD, 25 years
    SUE, 23 years
    CATH, 23 years
    ANNE, 23 years
    HELEN, 23 years

Note: It is essential that all the female parts in this play be interpreted by the one actress wearing the same costume, hairstyle, etc. That is, as far as the audience is concerned, there is in one important sense only one woman in the play. The male characters are naturally not aware of this and treat the women as different individuals. A costume change in the last scene for Helen would be acceptable.

PLAYWRIGHT'S NOTE

An expression of appreciation is due to David Kendall who first produced *White With Wire Wheels* at the University of Melbourne in September 1967. Valuable details from his original production have been assimilated into the text. I am similarly indebted to Lindzee Smith who directed the longer version of the play printed here for the Australian Performing Group at the Perth Festival, 1970.

Jack Hibberd

SCENE ONE

Early morning. A flat. A table and chairs.

MAL *enters. He is bleary-eyed, hung-over, and has just finished dressing—not too competently.*

MAL: Root my boot. What a night. [*Pause.*] Did we punish it last night. [*Pause.*] Water. That's what the system needs. Water. Let me at it.

> *He exits. The sound is heard of a tap running and* MAL *drinking numerous glasses of water. He returns.*

Got a tongue like a dog's dong. I feel like a fanny on fire. [*He sits and holds his head. Pause. He belches.*] Ahh. That's cleared the brain. Wonderful, wonderful water. [*Pause. He groans.*] Can't remember anything from nine in the evening till the moment I fell out of that bird's bed onto the cold lino. An unfortunate case of *coitus interruptus*. Drunk at the wheel. How I negotiated that passage I will never know. The old automatic pilot once again. [*Pause.*] Is it really all worth it? [*Pause.*] I think so. [*Pause.*] It must be. I always go back for more. Just as well I have a cast-iron constitution. Not to mention the stainless-steel stomach. I can count the number of times I've chucked on one hand. Wouldn't be two or three at the most. The last time was all over the dashboard of Don's new Daimler. What a monster act!

> *He laughs loudly and heartily. Pause and silence. He turns pale and looks nauseated, and dashes out. He is heard vomiting offstage. Pause. Silence.* ROD *enters. He has just collected the post and carries two magazines and a newspaper. He whistles gaily and sits down.* MAL, *pallid and seedy, slowly enters, wiping his mouth.*

ROD: [*looking at* MAL] Don't tell me!
MAL: Drop off.
ROD: [*gloating*] I refuse to believe it. I am flabbergasted.

> MAL *ignores him and sits down.*

Not Malcolm, the man who can count the number of times he's chundered on one hand. The man who loses his load but once a decade. Too much. It was only a couple of weeks ago that you

detonated over the dashboard of Don's new—
MAL: I know, I know. Don's new Daimler.
ROD: He's still scraping it off the walnut woodwork. Like scraping plankton off a hull. You lost a friend there, hooks.
MAL: Couldn't've happened to a better bloke. I wish I'd puked all over his poofta pants.
ROD: Charming. [*Pause.*] Well, chunder-chops, what'll it be? [*Holding up the magazines*] *Man Junior* or *Synchro-Mesh*?
MAL: *Man Junior*.
ROD: That would be more appropriate. But you'll have to be happy with *Synchro*.
MAL: Ta.
SIMON: [*entering*] Good morning, chaps. Great day for it.
ROD: Tremendous.

> SIMON *looks at* MAL, *who is reading, then turns quizzically to* ROD.

You'll never guess.
SIMON: No.
ROD: Yep.
SIMON: He's been for the big one?
ROD: And how. The kitchen is a sea of amber fluid.
SIMON: Pickled onions?
ROD: Indeed. And the green and gangrenous gherkin.

> *Pause.*

SIMON: [*to* MAL] How are you, chunder-chops?
MAL: Could you lower it to a roar?

> *Pause.* ROD *and* SIMON *exchange looks.*

SIMON: Think I'll get some milk. Hope there's not too much mess.
ROD: I'd be careful in there, chief. Step between the Squire's last squirt and all that.
SIMON: [*to* MAL] What on earth happened to you? Last I heard you were off for a quiet night at Sue's.
MAL: I succumbed.
SIMON: Well, suppose I'd better probe the pantry.

> SIMON *leaves.* MAL *and* ROD *read.*

ROD: Jesus. Get on to these for a set.
MAL: Eh?
ROD: This bird. Just have a look at those knockers.
MAL: [*peering*] A pair of pulverizers.
ROD: Udders to feed India. You could swing on those.

MAL: Very like the bird's I was with last night, actually.
ROD: What crap.
MAL: I'm for real.
ROD: [*ironically*] Sue?
MAL: No. Someone else. Shhh!
ROD: Who?
MAL: Think I'm going to tell you?

> SIMON *enters carrying two bottles of milk and a can of beer.*

SIMON: I've smelt worse. Don's new Daimler for instance.
ROD: What have you got there?
SIMON: A little surprise for Mal. [*To* MAL] There's only one thing that'll fix you, hooks.
MAL: [*engrossed in his magazine*] What?
SIMON: A nice, ice-cold can.
MAL: [*groaning*] I couldn't.
ROD: Not even you?
MAL: Not even me.
SIMON: [*opening the can*] Just the right temperature too.
ROD: Very important.
MAL: Take it away, or I'll unload in your lap.
SIMON: [*pouring a glass*] What a beautiful sound.
ROD: Hold your nose.
MAL: [*refusing to take the glass*] No.
ROD: Hold your snout and drink.
SIMON: Come on. It's the only way. After all, you're always recommending it to others.

> MAL *takes the glass, closes his eyes, holds his nose, and drinks. Cheers and applause from* ROD *and* SIMON.

Tremendous.
ROD: What a man.
SIMON: You can see it doing him good.
ROD: The colour's coming back into his cheeks.
SIMON: His eyes are regaining their former lustre.

> MAL *belches and beams.*

MAL: Better out than in. I can feel the vital juices at work already. Much improved.
SIMON: Great to hear.

> *They all return to their reading.* MAL *now reads the newspaper,*

SIMON *reads* Synchro. ROD *and* SIMON *drink milk from the bottle.*

MAL: What do you think of the new Cortina? [*Showing* ROD *and* SIMON] Nice-looking unit?
ROD: Not bad. Not bad at all.
MAL: Nice lines?
SIMON: Very classy.
MAL: Still, there are other jobs I'd prefer.
SIMON: Such as?
ROD: Such as this little job here. [*Displaying his magazine*] Just get a geek at those lines, gentlemen.
MAL: What a set.
SIMON: Impeccable.
ROD: Like watermelons.
SIMON: She's been tickled up.
ROD: Of course. Wouldn't you?
MAL: Could've been a cold snap.
ROD: I wouldn't mind a hot snap at that.
SIMON: [*reading*] 41-22-41.
MAL: Not bad for a Eurasian.

From left: Peter Corbett, Kevin Howard and Kristen Mann in the 1972 Independent Theatre production. From the Independent Theatre Collection, Mitchell Library, State Library of New South Wales. (Photo: Wal Easton)

ROD: Couldn't be a Eurasian. Not with a pair like that. She's a creole.
SIMON: Crap. Not with that broad beam.
MAL: She's a muleteer.
ROD: A what?
MAL: A muleteer. Half negro and half white. Noted for great bodies.
ROD: Something to do with pirates, I thought.

    Pause. They return to their reading.

MAL: Hey. Here's a shot of the Prime Minister swimming. All you can see above water is the tip of his snorkel.
ROD: Rude.
MAL: It says here he was looking for crabs.
ROD: [*looking at the photograph*] What a weapon.
SIMON: There's a '64 Rover here for five hundred.
MAL: I wouldn't pee on it.
SIMON: No one asked you to.
ROD: He'd chunder on it though.
MAL: Clever bastard.
ROD: Too clever for you, pinhead.
MAL: That would not be difficult in my present state of condition. [*Pause.*] Well. Tomorrow's the day, men.
ROD: For what?
MAL: The big day.
SIMON: I can hardly stand the suspense.
ROD: Don't tell me you're going to propose?
MAL: Eh?
SIMON: He's going to pop the question at last!
ROD: This calls for a celebration. More cans, Simon!
SIMON: Call for a keg!
ROD: Good old Sue. She's cracked it at last.
SIMON: What if she refuses?
MAL: Very funny.
ROD: Not much danger of that, eh Malco?
MAL: You're well wide of the mark.

    Pause.

ROD: Well, what's the big news? The event we've all been waiting for.
MAL: You'll find out soon enough.
ROD: When?
MAL: Later.
SIMON: Mal is upset.
MAL: You'll crap your daks when you find out.

ROD: I can hardly wait.
SIMON: Me too. When are we to be honoured with it?
MAL: Later today, if you're good.
ROD: I tremble with anticipation.
SIMON: The day will be long.
ROD: Just a hint?
SIMON: A snippet?
ROD: A morsel?
MAL: Go flog yourselves.
ROD: Charming.
SIMON: Lovely language.

   Pause.

ROD: Perhaps he's a father?
SIMON: Perhaps they're about to descend.
MAL: [*in a high-pitched voice*] There's nothing wrong with my tossle.

   They all laugh. The telephone is heard ringing. SIMON *leaps up and leaves.*

ROD: Simon's a bit toey.
MAL: Might be his boss.
ROD: Or his new girl.
MAL: Cath?
ROD: Wonder how he's making out there?
MAL: Rooty-toot-toot.
SIMON: [*entering*] It's for you, Mal.
MAL: Who is it?
SIMON: Give you one guess.
MAL: Banging Beatrice?
ROD: It'll be that lesbian from the Marriage Guidance Bureau.
SIMON: Wrong again.
MAL: Shirl the Shag?
SIMON: You know.
ROD: His one and only.
MAL: Jesus.

   MAL *leaves.*

ROD: [*after a pause*] How was she? Stacking on a turn?
SIMON: Not Sue. She's as placid as they come.
ROD: Lucky bastard. He's got it made.
SIMON: How'd he get his hooks into her?
ROD: Met her at a bucks' turn.

SIMON: You have to be joking.
ROD: It's true. She and one of her friends were discovered hiding in a wardrobe. They had hidden themselves there to hear all the ribald conversation and watch the tanning of Tony's testicles. We found them just in time and turfed them out. Or rather, Mal did. Being a cool operator, he took down Sue's particulars.
SIMON: The animal.
MAL: [*entering*] I heard that.
ROD: Well. How was she?
MAL: Who, Sue? No worries. No worries at all. Told her I ran into an old mate I hadn't seen for decades. Naturally enough we were forced to demolish a few jars, and before I knew where we were it was after midnight. The hours just slipped by.
ROD: We understand, Mal.
SIMON: We've heard it all before.
ROD: So has Sue, I suspect.
MAL: She was very glad of the early night.
ROD: She'll be waiting for you tonight like a caged animal.
SIMON: You'll be fighting *her* off instead of the reverse.
MAL: I hope so. I'm in no condition for a big wrassle.

    Pause.

SIMON: What's the time?
ROD: Half eight.
SIMON: Shit. I'd better make tracks. [*To* MAL] You coming to the pub tonight?
MAL: Can't say. I'll give you a ring at work.
SIMON: Anybody want the *Man Junior?*
MAL: Yeah. Me. I'll need it to pull me through the day.
ROD: Not feeling the best?
MAL: Not at my peak.
SIMON: Have another Dirty Dan. [*As he leaves*] See you.
ROD: See you at the pub. [*Pause.*] Who was she?
MAL: A female sword-swallower.
ROD: I know that. Her name.
MAL: I don't remember.
ROD: Crap.
MAL: I don't remember. I don't even remember the naughty. [*Pause.*] I woke up on the cold concrete floor beside her bed. She was leaning out and laughing at me with those enormous wobbling mammaries and wild black hair.
ROD: On her mammaries?

MAL: Where else? I'll never forget those nungers, and their red jelly-bean nipples. They'll haunt me for the rest of my life.
ROD: What the hell happened then?
MAL: She kissed me with her large liver lips, helped me to dress, stepped into some gear herself, and carried me down to the car. She wore jockettes. Don't you think that's odd for a bird? Black ones. Could've been a black jock-strap for all I know. How about that?
ROD: Did she drive you home?
MAL: Of course.
ROD: That's all?
MAL: She had a small waist.
ROD: What street was it?
MAL: And powerful forearms.
ROD: Covered in wild black hair. What street was it?
MAL: No idea. Give up, will you? [*Pause.*] Hey, I remember.
ROD: [*bored*] What?
MAL: Her name. It was Agatha.
ROD: You have to be joking.
MAL: I'm dead serious.
ROD: Count me out.
MAL: What's the matter? Why the sudden loss in interest?
ROD: She is called Agatha, has wild black hair all over her body, has powerful forearms, and wears a black jock-strap. Not my style at all.
MAL: What if I remember all the details?
ROD: Keep them to yourself, for Christ's sake. I have enough nightmares as it is. [*Pause.*] It's time I pushed off. Be five minutes late as it is. You coming?
MAL: In a minute. I might sink some of this milk.
ROD: Try and make the pub tonight. Don's coming.
MAL: How could I resist?
ROD: [*as he leaves*] See you.
MAL: Right.

   MAL *sits and drinks milk, reading* Man Junior.

SCENE TWO

A flat. A bed and sofa.

MAL *and* SUE *are dressing after making love. She is in bra and underpants, and is putting on her stockings.* MAL *is pulling on his trousers.*

MAL: [*after some time*] Hey, Sue.
SUE: Mmm?
MAL: Guess what?
SUE: What?
MAL: Tomorrow.
SUE: Tomorrow what?
MAL: I've a big surprise for you.
SUE: Yes? [*Putting on her dress*] What?
MAL: Come on. Can't you guess?
SUE: No idea.
MAL: No idea at all?
SUE: A few vague possibilities.
MAL: Think hard.
SUE: Is it very important?
MAL: Tremendously. For me anyway.

> *Pause.* MAL *walks upstage and does up his tie as if in front a mirror. She walks across and stands behind him, looking in the mirror over his shoulder and patting her hair into shape. Pause.*

SUE: Are you going to tell me?

> *She puts her arms around him from behind.*

[*Cooingly*] Please tell me. You look divine. Hold it, I'll just pat down your funny cocky's crest.

> *She laughs as she pats down a tuft of hair on his head. She resumes her embrace. Pause. He breaks the embrace and turns.*

MAL: You give up?
SUE: I give up.

> *He walks to the end of the bed and polishes his shoes with the bedspread.*

MAL: I've talked about it before, you know.
SUE: [*annoyed and restless*] That's a great help.
MAL: The big event for 1967. [*Pause.*] Tomorrow I pick up my new Valiant!

> *Pause.*

SUE: At last.
MAL: I can hardly wait. I've managed to wangle the morning off work. I walked straight up to the boss and told him I wanted to pick up a new

car. No lies. Just like that. Told him straight out. He was a bit surprised, but said I could have it off. Gave me the morning off, just like that. Beaut bloke. In fact he was very interested in the Valiant. Said he has always liked them. Drives a '62 Rover himself and has had good value from it. He's thinking of trading it in on something soon and wants to know how the Valiant performs. I've promised to take him for a burn when I've driven it in. It's a big chance for me to get to know him better. He's a bit stiff and remote, you know. Must take him to a pub. Loosen him up. With a few ales under his belt we could really click. I'm sure I won't get a moment's sleep tonight. I'll be outside those rooms at eight o'clock, flashing the big cheque book. I'm going to crawl over that bloody car—

SUE: Kiss the carburettor and tickle the tyres.

MAL: [*ignoring her*] Boy, the thing had better be flawless or I'll be back there tearing strips off the bastards. Actually the sales manager is a close mate of my old man's, so I shouldn't have any trouble. Not that you expect any problems in a new car.

Pause. SUE *sits down on the bed.*

SUE: Like a baby.

MAL: [*now very excited*] I've always wanted a bigger car. Not one of those American monsters. They're for the country, open roads and paddocks. Too big and difficult for the city traffic. Boy, the Valiant can really move. Have you seen the figures? Should be able to get to work in under fifteen minutes now. No trouble at all. I decided on a gear-change model. There's no real driving in an automatic. It's all done for you. A lazy man's invention for those who have no real love for cars and driving. It's a real art. Must show you the figures. Fuel consumption is not bad. Not as good as the Volksie of course. Can't expect that. I'll have to track down that Jap petrol from now on. [*Pause.*] Have a guess what colour I picked. This really gave me a lot of trouble.

SUE: Like choosing a name.

MAL: Have a guess.

SUE: Red.

MAL: Cut it out!

SUE: Black.

MAL: What?! And look like an undertaker or Toorak tycoon?

SUE: Thought you'd like that. Blue.

MAL: Which blue?

SUE: Pastel blue, baby blue, egg-shell blue, sky blue, eye blue—

MAL: No! Too weak. Something stronger, more masculine.
SUE: Royal blue.
MAL: Deep-sea blue.
SUE: But that has green in it.
MAL: Yes, it has got a touch of green.

Pause. He laughs.

SUE: What's so funny?
MAL: It's not blue at all.
SUE: Very funny.
MAL: It's white.
SUE: White?!
MAL: White with wire wheels.
SUE: How flash can you get.
MAL: No, it's just right. A study in style. Lots of character.
SUE: You will have to wear dark suits all the time. Think of the colour scheme.
MAL: Don't be stupid. Any outfit will go with it. Pale summer-weight suits and large Italian sunglasses. Can't you see me? As cool as a cucumber.
SUE: As funny as cork.
MAL: A study in style.
SUE: Like a pig in shit.
MAL: Rolling down to Rio.
SUE: As proud as Peter.
MAL: Rudolph Valentino.
SUE: Errol Flynn setting sail for the high seas. When can I see it?
MAL: Any time.
SUE: Saturday?
MAL: No hope. I'm taking six of the blokes up to a beer garden in the hills. It's all arranged. Strictly a day for the chaps.
SUE: Couldn't you fit me in?
MAL: Come off it, Sue. Don't prove difficult.
SUE: Well, if that's the situation…
MAL: I'll be around soon.
SUE: Thanks. [*Pause. She rises from the bed.*] When you had me guessing before, for a moment, just for a moment, I thought you were going to propose.

She smiles sheepishly but is firm and feminine underneath it all.

MAL: Don't be sick.
SUE: I don't think it's sick.

MAL: Well I do!

SUE: I couldn't help myself.

MAL: Don't I know that. Every time we're together lately you bring the subject around to that. Can't you think of anything else?!

Pause. She sits on the bed again.

Listen, Sue, I've explained to you before, I'm not ready for marriage. It's remote, as far as I'm concerned. As remote as death. I've got my career to think of. I have to establish myself.

SUE: Damn your career for the moment. If you love me as you say you do, surely you must want to get married.

MAL: It's not as simple as that.

SUE: All right, it's complex. But it's been complex for three years now and it's not getting any simpler. Not for me anyway. It gets more complex for me every month that goes by. You've been sleeping with me for three years now and still not a sign, nothing to cling to but 'I love you' every now and again. I need more. Can't you understand?

MAL: No, I bloody well can't. It's just a stupid nesting instinct that should be ignored for a while. I treat you well. I take you out. We have a good time. I give you stacks of affection.

SUE: There comes a time…

MAL: What?

SUE: When that isn't enough, and when it isn't enough for a long time it becomes bloody nothing.

MAL: What sort of crap is this?

SUE: I've had enough. I'm calling it all off, Mal.

MAL: What did you say?

SUE: I don't want to see you again.

MAL: Are you serious?

SUE: No. It's one of my little jokes, Mal.

Pause. She stands.

MAL: You're dropping me!

SUE: I don't see much point in going on.

He seizes her wrist and twists it viciously.

MAL: [*leaning over her*] Just you try it. Just you try it.

SUE: Stop twisting my arm. Do you think you can twist a change of mind out of me?

MAL: [*letting go of her wrist*] You stupid bitch! [*Pause.*] I bloody well ought to beat some sense into you. You can't walk out on me like this—

SUE: What are you going to tell your friends?
MAL: Give me a bit more time—
SUE: You've had more than enough.
MAL: Give me some more time. I'll work it out.

> *He lifts her up from the bed. She stands rigidly before him. He puts his arms around her and draws her to him.*

Come on, Sue. Cheer up. You're just a little depressed. Sorry for abusing you like that and twisting your arm. [*Cuddling her*] Let's make up.

> *He tickles her and tries to kiss her. She avoids him, then submits, but impassively.*

That's the way, Sue. That's the girl I know. You'll be a lot better tomorrow. Listen, I'll call off my night at the pub tomorrow night and we'll head out to dinner, then take in a show. Agreed? You'll see the Valiant then. We'll burn down to the beach afterwards, listen to the wireless, and be romantic. The sea, the moon, the fresh air. A new lease of life. Right, Sue?

> *Pause.*

SUE: [*walking away*] No, Mal. It's not right. I meant what I said. I know, I feel it.
MAL: What do you feel? There's only one thing you feel. [*Pause.*] All right. Go to hell, then. You're not that bloody attractive that you can toss men around. I don't want to see you again either. You've been getting on my nerves lately—hints, suggestions, whinges. You don't know when you're on to a good thing. [*He walks over and picks up his coat from the sofa.*] You'll regret this one day.

> *He leaves.*

SCENE THREE

Same scene.

SIMON *and* CATH *enter.*

SIMON: Great film, eh Cath?
CATH: Superb.
SIMON: [*sitting on the sofa*] Like to see it again?
CATH: Love to.
SIMON: Next week then.

CATH: Agreed.

> *Pause.* CATH *sits.*

SIMON: Pity about Mal and his girlfriend not being able to make it. I wonder what they were up to? Getting amongst it, I suppose. Have you met Sue, his girlfriend, yet?

CATH: Not that I can recall.
SIMON: You'd remember. She's a real doll. Beautiful figure. Unique. I envy that bastard.
CATH: Careful, you'll make me jealous.
SIMON: Not a chance. You're unique too.
CATH: But different?
SIMON: Exactly. Variety is the spice of life. [*Pause.*] Still, I wouldn't mind a stab at her some time. No chance there, however. They've been going out together for three years. Both very happy. A perfect arrangement for Mal.
CATH: She sounds very nice.
SIMON: Unique.
CATH: I'd like to meet her.
SIMON: You will. No worries there. The two of you'll get on like a house on fire.

> *Pause.*

CATH: [*standing*] Would you like some coffee?
SIMON: Love some.
CATH: It'll have to be Percy's Perfect Grind. Instant variety.
SIMON: You want to invest in a grinder.
CATH: [*as she leaves*] That's what I keep telling myself.
SIMON: Very handy weapon. [*Pause.*] Jesus. I'm all washed out. Very moving film. [*Pause. Raising his voice*] Great film, eh Cath? Full of action, colour, scenery and romance. Continually entertaining. That's what I liked about it. Never a dull moment. How about the symbolism of when he held that lighted match. The Flame of Life eating into his anatomy. The control of mind over body. Too much. Always presenting another side of his character, yet telling a story, and what a story! [*Pause.*] Hey, wasn't the music exciting?
CATH: [*offstage*] Devastating!
SIMON: That's the word. Had me on the edge of my seat all night. [*Pause. Reflectively*] Amazing for classical music.
CATH: [*offstage*] How do you like your coffee? I've forgotten!
SIMON: [*laughing*] How could you?! Strong and straight, like a real man.

A round of applause is heard from CATH.

Thank you. That's me.

CATH: [*offstage*] Nearly ready!

>   SIMON *lights up a cigarette, then picks up a newspaper and reads. He whistles gaily.*

SIMON: Not much else on. Seen most of the musicals. Here's a rude Continental film. Must see that.

CATH: [*entering with the coffee*] You would.

SIMON: So I'm made for it. [*Pause.*] Thanks. [*He takes his coffee and sips.*] It's just that I love women. Really appreciate them.

>   *He puts down his coffee and blows a smoke ring through which he pokes a finger as* CATH *sits down and sips her coffee.*

CATH: The trouble with those sort of films is that they are never rude and—

SIMON: Crap!

CATH: Well, they just aren't.

SIMON: That's only a female point of view.

CATH: Therefore 'crap'. They're never erotic.

SIMON: I tell you, some of them are. You're not a man, you wouldn't know. [*Pause.*] Now, if they had similar shows for the females, I'm sure you'd be aroused.

CATH: I'm not so sure.

SIMON: Well, I am sure. Not all of them, naturally. You have to discriminate. Some of them are takes. [*Pause.*] Hell, what I could do with some of those Continental women. The French birds, for example.

CATH: [*smiling*] They might be able to teach you something.

SIMON: They might. But it wouldn't be a one-way performance. Women are basically all the same. I'm sure our Australian men have something to offer. I think we are a more inventive race than a lot of people give us credit for. [*Long pause.*] How's work?

CATH: I don't like it. I don't like work, employment or a career. It has no point. It would only have a point if—

SIMON: You don't want to look at it that way. I don't like work, but I've trained myself to adapt to it, to get on top of it and always look ahead, create an objective and go for it, tooth and nail. You mustn't let your emotions get in your way. Stand on them. Crush them. Then you find yourself accepting it all. You're too emotional, Cath.

CATH: You think so?

SIMON: Positive. [*Pause. He finishes off his coffee.*] Did I tell you that I

could get into the head office soon?
CATH: No.
SIMON: Well—
CATH: Would you like some more coffee?
SIMON: Terrific.

She walks out with his cup. He lights up another cigarette.

Where was I? [*Raising his voice*] Oh yes, about the head office. I've been putting out a few feelers lately. The blokes where I work at the moment aren't much help, so I took one of the senior executives from the head office out to dinner the other night. I've met him a few times at various functions. He's a bit hard to get to know, but the dinner worked out well. Took him to one of those pubs with a floorshow, bit of strip, song and dance, you know the sort of thing. He really enjoyed himself. Get him away from his wife for a while. Nice woman, but a bit house-bound. He has five kids. They must get the poor bastard down.

She returns with the coffee.

Naturally the conversation turned to work and the firm. With a few more beers under our respective belts I had no worries about probing him with regard to my chances. Of course he had to be discreet, but he hinted that it wouldn't be too long at all.
CATH: For what?
SIMON: Haven't you been listening? The head office of course! Things should really start to move then, bigger salary, all expenses paid, an ear to the Stock Exchange. I'll be glad to be out of that dead-end place in the suburbs. Can hardly wait. [*Pause.*] Did you know Mal was buying a new Valiant?
CATH: No.
SIMON. Picking it up tomorrow.
CATH: A big day for him?
SIMON. Too right. I should be envious, but I've got my eye on something different.
CATH: A motorbike and sidecar?
SIMON: No! Get with it. A '62. Rover. Something more conservative, solid, a touch of class.
CATH: Mature.
SIMON: That's right. There's something too flash and gangsterish about the Valiant. He's ordered a white one with wire wheels, just the kind I would've ordered if I was going for a Valiant. What colour would you have chosen?

CATH: Red. Rooster red.
SIMON: What?!
CATH: Something passionate.
SIMON: Typical woman. You're not picking a dress. [*He moves closer to her.*] Talking of dresses. I like that dress you're wearing tonight.
CATH: Thank you.
SIMON: Did you make it yourself?

CATH: Yes.
SIMON: [*ogling her*] Very good.

> *He puts his arm around her.*

Never seen that style before. It really does something for your figure.
CATH: I'm being charmed.
SIMON: I wouldn't say it unless I meant it.

> *He has a last draw on his cigarette, then stubs it out. He turns to* CATH *and begins to stroke her hair.*

I'm getting very fond of you, Cath.

> *He kisses her lightly and quickly on the lips. She looks intently into his face.*

Don't you believe me?
CATH: Of course.
SIMON: Beaut. Can I see a lot more of you?
CATH: That's up to you.
SIMON: Don't worry about me. I'm going to plague you.
CATH: Nasty word.
SIMON: Haunt you.
CATH: Just as nasty.
SIMON: Hunt you.
CATH: Oooooh!

> *They laugh. He looks quickly at his watch, then moves in for another kiss.*

What time is it?
SIMON: [*surprised*] Oh, about midnight. [*Pause.*] What a time to—?
CATH: —ask for the time. You looked at your watch.
SIMON: Just a habit.

> *He moves in for another kiss and does so with some enthusiasm. She is more impassive.*

You kiss very nicely.

He strokes her neck and shoulders. He kisses her on the neck. She responds by caressing him on the neck and holding firmly. He breaks the embrace and leans back, stretching his limbs, his gaze fixed on her face.

Let's go to bed.
CATH: No.

He leans towards her, solicitously and affectionately putting his arms around her. He tickles her. She struggles more than wriggles.

SIMON: Come on, Cath, let's have some fun.
CATH: I can't.
SIMON: Why not? [*Pause.*] Is there some special reason at the moment?
CATH: No, not what you think.

He attempts to kiss her again. They struggle.

SIMON: Come on, Cath. I love you.
CATH: [*grimly*] No.
SIMON: Listen, you've got no worries about you-know-what. I'm always prepared.
CATH: Like a pimply boy scout. You don't understand.
SIMON: You're serious?
CATH: Of course I am.

Pause.

SIMON: [*with an uneasy shifting of his hands*] Well, that's that, I suppose. Pity. [*Smiling at her*] I'm in great form tonight.
CATH: How do you know?
SIMON: I can feel it.

Pause.

CATH: I thought you may have had a quick seduction earlier in the evening.

Pause.

SIMON: Some other time, eh?
CATH: [*standing*] Of course.
SIMON: [*standing*] Well. [*Looking at his watch*] Suppose I must be off.
CATH: You don't have to go, you know.
SIMON: No. I really must be off. Have to be at work early tomorrow. Too many late nights recently.

She gathers the cups and leaves. He lights a cigarette and blows smoke rings. Pause. She re-enters.

Must be off. Goodnight, Cath.
CATH: Goodnight. Thanks for the night out.

SIMON: [*as he leaves, he blows* CATH *a kiss*] A pleasure.

SCENE FOUR

Same scene.

ROD *sits on the sofa with his feet up, reading a paper. Pause.* ANNE *enters. She stands and stares at* ROD. *Pause.*

ANNE: What's wrong with you tonight?
ROD: [*surprised*] Nothing. Nothing at all, Anne.
ANNE: There is. I can sense it.
ROD: Pure imagination.
ANNE: I'd say intuition.
ROD: Intuition, imagination. All the same thing. What have I done? How am I different?
ANNE: It's nothing you've said or done. It's a feeling I have.
ROD: Women and their feelings!
ANNE: They exist.
ROD: I don't doubt that.
ANNE: Well?
ROD: Ignore them.

> *Pause. She sits down.*

Are you off colour?
ANNE: No.
ROD: You look like you've got a headache.
ANNE: Thanks. [*Pause.*] I feel perfectly well, actually.
ROD: Great to hear. [*Moving closer to her*] You had me worried. How about one?

> *She kisses him lightly on the lips.*

Hey, that was a bit mean!

> *He stands and takes her by the hand.*

Come over to the bed and I'll give you a real kiss.

> *He leads her to the bed.*

ANNE: Can I take it?

> ROD *lies on the bed, flexes his muscles in an exaggerated fashion, and makes exuberant kissing sounds as she slips off her shoes. She lies down and they kiss for some time.*

ROD: Ahhhh! That's an improvement.

> *She sits up, preoccupied.*

See, you were wrong.

> *She stands and turns to adjust her hair as if in front of a mirror. He watches her.*

I'm no different tonight to what I'll ever be. Ha! Talk about imaginitis. All you needed was some affection.

> *He watches her with great interest for a response as she finishes with her hair and puts on her shoes.*

The cure for all evils. [*Pause. He lights up a cigarette.*] Is there an ashtray around?

ANNE: No. It's in the kitchen. I'll get it.

> *She walks off.*

ROD: [*raising his voice*] It's always in the kitchen. You must wash it five times a day, or is it a special kitchen ashtray, not fitting in with the decor of the sitting room?

ANNE: [*entering with a kitchen-tidy*] That's right.

> *He doesn't notice the kitchen-tidy as he lies looking at the ceiling and blowing clouds of smoke into the air.*

[*Placing the kitchen-tidy on the floor beside him*] The ashtray has arrived. [*Pause.*] Would you like to use it?

ROD: Sure.

> *He leans over with the cigarette and as he does so she suddenly springs the lid of the kitchen-tidy open by pressing the foot pedal.*

Hey!

ANNE: It can also be used as a spittoon and a receptacle for your shoes.

ROD: Big joke. What's the point?

ANNE: You're clumsy and you're obvious.

> *He taps his cigarette over the orifice of the kitchen-tidy. She turns and walks off, releasing the mechanism and so trapping his hand in the kitchen-tidy.*

ROD: Very smart!

> *She sits on the sofa, looking back at* ROD *as he extracts his hand. Long pause.*

Hey, did you know Mal was buying a new car?

ANNE: I think you mentioned it before, or someone could have.

ROD: It's a new Valiant.

ANNE: That's right. Deep-sea blue, isn't it?
ROD: No! It's white. That was his second choice.
ANNE: I forgot.
ROD: With wire wheels. [*Pause.*] He's doing well at his job too. Did you know that?
ANNE: No.
ROD: Moving into the head office soon. Really got the clues, that boy. Heading for the big time. [*He prises open the lid of the kitchen-tidy and drops some ash in. Pause.*] No doubt about it.
ANNE: Well, you're not exactly losing ground.
ROD: True. But I still have a long way to go. Now I know the ropes thoroughly, there'll be no stopping me. A man with a purpose. [*Pause.*] What were we doing next Saturday?
ANNE: Going over to meet Simon's new girlfriend at Sue's place.
ROD: The beautiful creatures!
ANNE: Have you arranged it?
ROD: No. It's all off. Mal is taking a carload of us up the hills for a booze-up. Six of us in the Valiant. Strictly a day for the chaps.
ANNE: Well, don't get too drunk and crash the car.
ROD: No worries there. Mal is one of the most talented drunken drivers I've ever come across. I've seen him, pissed to the eyeballs, do the most amazing things—beautifully judged cornering and controlled broadsides. Were you there the time he roared between a tram and a parked car? [*Gesturing enthusiastically*] There just wasn't room! I screamed at him not to try it. But he ignored me and bored straight on. Not a scratch. Must've been a quarter of an inch to spare on each side. Bloody amazing performance. He should be in the racing game. I've told him numerous times.
ANNE: I wish he wouldn't.
ROD: Why?
ANNE: I get terribly frightened.
ROD: Don't be weak.
ANNE: I don't want to end up a cripple.
ROD: He's quite safe really. I know. Never blotted his copybook. I feel much safer with him than my old man who thrashes around the city at a death-defying speed—thirty miles per hour. In a new Jaguar. What do you think of that?! You'd think he was running it on wop juice. [*Pause. He rises from the bed, bringing the kitchen-tidy with him, walking to the sofa.*] Anne, I've got something to tell you.
ANNE: What?
ROD: [*coldly*] I'm calling it off.

ANNE: You're what?
ROD: [*standing by the side of the sofa*] I don't want to see you again. I'm calling it off.

> *Pause. They exchange stares. She stands.*

ANNE: Just like that.
ROD: [*aggressively*] Just like that. I don't want to get mixed up in any long affair at the moment.

> *Pause.*

ANNE: But why? Why? Why?
ROD: You're getting too fond of me. I think it's better to call it off now when it won't hurt you as much as it would if I called it off later on.
ANNE: That's a bit lame.
ROD: No scenes, please.

> *He dashes his cigarette into the kitchen-tidy now at his feet.*

ANNE: Damn you, Rod.

> *He shrugs.*

It's obvious I've been very fond of you, in love with you, for some months now. I can't swallow that.
ROD: You'll have to. It's all finished.

> *He lights another cigarette.*

ANNE: You've enjoyed me for three months and now you pull out.
ROD: It's not like that at all. I'm thinking of myself as well. It won't hurt me as much now as it would later on. It's easier all 'round. Don't you see? [*Pause. Shouting*] Do I have to go into all my motives? Do I have to go down on my knees and beg you to let me go? Beg forgiveness for all the times we enjoyed each other? No. What *do* you want? [*Pause.*] It's my own bloody life!
ANNE: [*calmly*] That's the whole trouble.
ROD: What do you mean by that? [*Pause.*] I aim to make the best of it. It's just not convenient at the moment. To hell with it! I'm not going into it all. I don't have to. I've made up my mind and there's nothing you can do about it. I have my reasons, don't worry. I just don't want to see you again. Is that clear? [*Pause.*] To be honest, I'm sick of you. You just don't interest me anymore. You bore me. I may even hate your guts. When this happens, I naturally just move on. Simple as that. What else can you expect me to do? [*Pause.*] Well, I don't see much point in staying.
ANNE: [*sitting on the sofa*] Yes, go on, run off, run away.
ROD: I'm not running away from anything!

ANNE: I think so.
ROD: What?
ANNE: From…

She pauses.

ROD: From what?! Come on, tell me. As if you knew or could know. That's old hat, that sort of line—trying to make me feel guilty.
ANNE: That's not necessary.

ROD: Of course it isn't. It would be hypocritical to go on with it the way I feel at the moment.
ANNE: I'm proud of you.
ROD: Don't be bitchy.
ANNE: After all, you could've written me a letter. The easy way out.
ROD: Don't be bloody silly. You've got the message. Whether or not I loved you, you'd be a millstone around my neck.
ANNE: That would make two.
ROD: There are two sides to all this. You're not the only one who has problems, you know.
ANNE: You need your independence?
ROD: That's one corny way of putting it.
ANNE: You need it once every six months or so.
ROD: I need it all the time. [*He stands in front of her and speaks slowly.*] I just don't like you anymore.
ANNE: And you never really have.
ROD: That's a lie and you know it!
ANNE: You've told me otherwise?
ROD: Yes, and I'm not going to stand here and be cross-examined.

He moves away.

ANNE: You're in charge of the scene.
ROD: All right, you're upset. Be upset by yourself! I'm going before the tears start to roll.

He starts to walk off.

ANNE: Can I have a cigarette?

She rises. He turns and gives her a cigarette. He lights it for her. She looks him in the face. He ignores her and exits. She stands for some time smoking. She then turns to the kitchen-tidy and slowly raises the lid with the foot pedal. She taps her cigarette above it.

SCENE FIVE

The flat. Same as Scene One. Table and chairs.

MAL *and* SIMON *enter.*

MAL: [*sitting down*] What sort of night did you have?
SIMON: [*joining him*] Not too bad. Not too bad at all.

MAL: How was the film?
SIMON: Marvellous. One of the best. No sex in it, however. [*Pause.*] Not a female.
MAL: Well, he was a queer, you know.
SIMON: [*shaking his head*] Not a female.

Pause.

MAL: How was Cath?
SIMON: Beaut.
MAL: Watch yourself, Romeo. You'll go down in flames.
SIMON: Not me.
MAL: Did you crack it?
SIMON: No. But I've got her all lined up. She was having her monthly tonight.
MAL: Didn't think that would worry you.
SIMON: [*lighting a cigarette*] She's a bit shy.
MAL: [*laughing*] Come on, you're just not smooth enough.
SIMON: You're not so smooth, being hooked with the one woman for years.
MAL: I've indulged in a bit on the side.
SIMON: [*mockingly*] You haven't!
MAL: You knew about Val, Bernadette and Mandy.
SIMON: All obvious knocks. No smoothness involved there.
MAL: You should talk. What about the line-up of harlots you've inflicted us with?! Roaring nymphos. The last one left tampons and smelly underwear all over the bathroom. We had liquid and unsalted scrambled eggs every morning for a week, as well as bad breath and green teeth.
SIMON: An opportunity at last!
MAL: For what?
SIMON: To tell you what your best friend should always be the first to tell you. [*Pause. With an air of being confidential*] You have bad breath too. Like the local tip.

MAL: You bastard!
SIMON: You had to be told. You just gave me the chance. [*Pause*.] And Sue has such sweet breath.
MAL: Why don't you shut your mouth?
SIMON: Fair's fair. You were slinging off at Gloria.
MAL: Jesus, Simon, she was hopeless.
SIMON: I was desperate. Randy enough for anything that looked vaguely human.
MAL: You should've lined up Penny, the camp mule. At least she can cook, and is clean.

SIMON: Don't you believe it! I copped a dose of the clap off her last time.
MAL: What?!
SIMON: True as I'm here.
MAL: I was going to line her up for a weekend down the coast soon. That finishes that.
SIMON: Try it. Fish hooks and hot lead in your pencil. You'll pay the penalty.
MAL: I've been penalised before, don't worry.
SIMON: A real man.

    Pause.

MAL: Talking of real men, I wonder how Rod went tonight.
SIMON: I'd forgotten. He was breaking it off with Anne tonight. I wouldn't think he'd have any trouble. He's a very smooth operator.
MAL: Talk his way out of anything.
SIMON: If I know Rod, he'll be a free man tonight. [*Pause*.] Hey, did I tell you about taking one of the chief executives out the other night and oiling him up?
MAL: Yes.
SIMON: Should be in the head office soon.
MAL: You deserve it. I've managed to get on the right side of my boss over the Valiant. Taking him for a burn soon. He wants a change from his Rover and is interested in the Valiant. Must be in top driving form that afternoon. All stops out for the big impression.
SIMON: What year Rover is it?
MAL: About a '62.
SIMON: Good. Keep me in touch. I want to buy one. Must be in perfect condition.
MAL: No worries there. It's a gem. He has it tuned like a musical instrument.
SIMON: Great to hear.

ROD *enters.*

Here he is!
MAL: Rudolph Valentino!
SIMON: Rhubarb Vaselino!

They laugh. ROD *sits down. Pause.*

MAL: How did it go tonight? You're a bit quiet.
ROD: No trouble at all. I just broke it to her calmly and firmly. Dealt her out the usual story.
SIMON: How did she take it?
ROD: A bit hysterical.

MAL: Weeping.
SIMON: Pleading.
ROD: Demanding.
MAL: She didn't understand?
SIMON: How could you?!
ROD: Don't do it, she said.
SIMON: Pity. She was really very nice.
MAL: I thought you would've had more trouble with her.
ROD: Well, I had to be tough towards the finish.
MAL: In complete control.
SIMON: Dictating the play.
ROD: Full points.

They all laugh. Pause.

SIMON: How about a bottle?
MAL: Too right.
ROD: Please.

SIMON *walks out.* ROD *lights a cigarette.*

That's that. I'm a free man once again.
MAL: Any ideas?
ROD: Not a one. Just wait and see what turns up.
MAL: Not if I know you. You'll have your hooks into something pretty quick.
ROD: No. I'm off women for a while.
MAL: They'll never understand.

SIMON *returns with beer and glasses.*

Rod is off the women.
SIMON: [*setting down the beer and glasses*] I don't believe it. You aren't called 'The Pump' for nothing.

ROD: It's true. My well has dried up. Nothing to pump.
SIMON: [*opening a very cold bottle with a snap*] Do you hear that?!
MAL: A beautiful sound.
ROD: Words couldn't describe it.
SIMON: [*pouring the beer*] An Elixir of Love. [*Pause.*] Well, cheers.

They raise their glasses and drink.

ROD: Christ, I needed that.
SIMON: Ahhhh.

Pause.

MAL: I had an eventful night too.
ROD: How come?
MAL: Sue and I had a fight. I called it off.
SIMON: What?! Why didn't you tell me?
MAL: Didn't feel like it.
ROD: After all this time. What happened?
MAL: She's been giving me the shits lately. Whingeing and insinuating about marriage. I've just had a gutful of it. Told her where to get off.

MAL *drinks.*

ROD: You too?
MAL: Me too.
SIMON: Jesus, three years, then bang.
MAL: It had to happen soon.
ROD: Just when you were buying the Valiant too.
SIMON: I thought she had you.
MAL: Not a chance. It had developed into a habit.
SIMON: A very pleasant habit.
ROD: [*enthusiastically*] She was really beautiful.
SIMON: Gorgeous.
MAL: [*quickly*] I know, I know. I'll get some more beer.

MAL *walks off.*

ROD: He should have pulled out earlier.
SIMON: That's easier said than done.
ROD: You have to do it.
SIMON: I would have found it difficult with Sue.

MAL *returns with another bottle.*

You must have been cheesed-off to do it, Mal.
MAL: I was.

SIMON *opens the bottle with the same effect.*

ROD: He's done it again!
MAL: Nice action there, feller.
ROD: A real sense of style.
SIMON: [*pouring more beer*] Well, I've no intention of seeing Cath again. Told her I'd take her out. She'll never see me again.
MAL: But you told me you had her all lined up.
SIMON: I did. So what? I'm not mad for it.
MAL: But why?
SIMON: She doesn't interest me.
ROD: So, we're all in the same boat. The first time for years. Let's drink to that.

They all drink. Pause.

MAL: Did you know beautiful Basil was moving out?
SIMON: No.
ROD: When?
MAL: Today or tomorrow. I saw him last night with some of his mates at the Universal Joint. He's moving in with Neil.
ROD: How cosy.
SIMON: Hey, I saw a girl looking over his flat yesterday. She must be moving in. A bloody doll too. Fabulous. Fancy getting rid of that weak bastard Basil and scoring a woman.
ROD: Are you sure?
SIMON: Yes, positive. No doubt about it. It's a good flat. She must take it.
MAL: Bags her.
SIMON: I saw her first. She's mine.
ROD: She belongs to all of us at the moment. Or rather, doesn't belong to any of us. We must be accurate. Anyway, she probably has a muscle-bound boyfriend.
MAL: I'll nail him.
SIMON: You?!
MAL: I can handle myself.
ROD: [*knowingly*] We all know that.
MAL: [*peeved*] Ha, ha, haaa.
SIMON: Anyway, keep your eyes peeled.
MAL: Sure thing.
ROD: Sure thing.

Pause.

MAL: I'm off to bed. Have to be up early tomorrow. Picking up the Valiant.
SIMON: Capitalist!
MAL: Envy written all over his face.

SIMON: What?! Of a common Valiant?
MAL: It'd crap on a Rover any time.
ROD: [*ironically*] Good point.
MAL: Have you seen the figures?
SIMON: What figures?
MAL: In the latest copy of *Synchro-Mesh*!
SIMON: You don't believe them, do you?
MAL: Of course. Why not?
SIMON: Get a grip of yourself.
MAL: [*pointing at* SIMON] You be careful. You may not be included in the drive to the hills on Saturday.
SIMON: [*getting down on his knees before* MAL; *meekly*] No! Please, not that! Don't do it to me, Mal!

MAL stands and starts to circle the table. He pretends he is driving a car, and makes the sounds (gear changes, etc.) appropriate to hard driving.

ROD: When can we see it, Mal?
MAL: [*between gear changes*] Tomorrow night, if you're lucky!

After another circuit, MAL *exits.*

SIMON: [*still on his knees; as* MAL *leaves*] Take it away, Mal!
ROD: Think I'll drive off to bed, too.
SIMON: What are you driving tonight?
ROD: The old hot-rod! No, no! An orange De Soto!

ROD now revs up and takes off around the table. SIMON *flags him down as he passes in front of the table and roars off the stage.* SIMON, *who has been laughing, settles into silence. Still on his knees, he systematically drains all the cans and glasses on the table. Pause. He belches.*

SIMON: One cylinder job. [*Pause. Leering*] Must con that new girl.

He walks offstage on his knees.

SCENE SIX

A milk bar. A table, chairs and a counter. The counter consists of a shelf against an upstage wall. There is a hole or aperture above the shelf in the centre of the wall.

SIMON *leans on the counter drinking a milkshake. Pause.*

SIMON: Not a bad sort of day for this time of the year.
VOICE: [*through the aperture; gravel in quality*] Not bad at all.
SIMON: We could do with a few more of these.

   Pause.

VOICE: Sign of an early spring.
SIMON: Good for business.

   Pause.

VOICE: Gives you a new lease of life.
SIMON: True.

   Pause. HELEN *enters and walks to the counter.* SIMON *steps aside.*

HELEN: Glass of lemonade with a straw, please.
VOICE: Right.

   Pause. The lemonade and straw appear in a hand at the aperture.

HELEN: [*taking the lemonade*] How much is that?
VOICE: [*sexily*] Nothing for you, lady.
HELEN: Thank you.

   She sits down at the table and drinks.

SIMON: [*turning to* HELEN] Excuse me, but you're not the girl that has moved in next door?
HELEN: [*shaking her head*] No.
SIMON: [*advancing*] But I'm sure it was you I saw looking over the flat the other day.

   Pause. HELEN *is preoccupied with her drink and doesn't reply.*

   [*Puzzled; hesitatingly*] Er, mind if I join you?
HELEN: [*between sips*] Not at all.
SIMON: Thirsty?

   He sits down.

HELEN: [*finishing her lemonade*] No.

   Pause.

SIMON: It was you, wasn't it?
HELEN: [*smiling*] Maybe.
SIMON: [*puzzled*] Maybe?
HELEN: Maybe.
SIMON: [*laughing; uncomfortable*] Yes or no?
HELEN: [*smiling*] Yes and no.
SIMON: [*not to be denied*] A friend of ours, Basil, lived up there.
HELEN: Oh yes. A nice chap if I remember rightly.

SIMON: Yes. Very nice. [*Pause.*] You have moved into his flat then?
HELEN: [*vaguely*] What's your name?
SIMON: Oh, sorry. Simon. I live with two rogues called Mal and Rod.
HELEN: [*half to herself*] Pall Mall and Hot Rod.
SIMON: What?
HELEN: Nothing.
SIMON: Like another one?

>HELEN *shakes her head.*

[*Rising*] Think I'll sock down another milkshake. Need a lot of milk to keep me in trim. I used to drink three pints a day at school. No stopping me.
HELEN: That must account for your superb build.

>SIMON *laughs.* HELEN *smiles. Pause.*

SIMON: [*rattled*] Er, on second thoughts, don't think I will have one. Mal is knocking up a roast tonight. Will have to save myself for that. [*Pause. He sits down.*] Not a bad sort of day for this time of the year.
VOICE: Good for business.

>*Pause.* SIMON *is annoyed.*

Sign of an early autumn.
SIMON: Hey, you wouldn't like to come to dinner tonight, would you?
VOICE: Love to.
HELEN: [*shaking her head, smiling firmly*] Sorry.
SIMON: Some other time then?
HELEN: [*shaking her head*] Yes. [*Pause. Rising*] Excuse me, must order a taxi.
SIMON: [*rising*] Hey, I can give you a—
HELEN: [*walking to the counter*] Thanks all the same. You must have your roast.
SIMON: But…
HELEN: [*at the aperture*] Excuse me.

>*Pause. Silence.*

SIMON: Are you going anywhere in particular?
HELEN: Nowhere in particular.

>*Pause.* SIMON *sits down, defeated for the moment.*

Excuse me.
VOICE: What can I do for you, lady?
HELEN: Could you order a taxi for me?
VOICE: A pleasure.

Pause. Cigarette smoke is blown through the aperture. SIMON *lights up a cigarette and eyes* HELEN *off from behind.*

Any particular firm?
HELEN: Express Motors.
VOICE: Any place in particular?
HELEN. Nowhere in particular. [*Pause.*] How much do I owe you?
VOICE: [*sexily*] Nothing for you, lady.
HELEN: [*turning away*] Thank you.

HELEN *leans against the counter. Pause.*

SIMON: [*desperate*] Smoke?

HELEN: No thanks.

The hairy arm appears through the aperture and gropes around for a while, then returns.

SIMON: [*rising*] You may as well come over here and rest your weary limbs while waiting for the taxi; they often take a while in this area.
HELEN: [*walking across*] All right.
SIMON: [*sitting down*] Boy, did we hit it last night.
HELEN: What? The milk?
SIMON: [*laughing*] No. The booze.
HELEN: Any particular occasion?
SIMON: Yes. Mal was picking up a new Valiant today. Oh, and a few other things happened too. Rod broke it off with his girlfriend, for example.
HELEN: Is that a cause for celebration?
SIMON: We thought so.
HELEN: He'd struck a blow for freedom?
SIMON: Yes. That's right. [*Pause.*] Anyway, Rod's love troubles probably don't interest you. Nothing more boring than talking about people you don't know.
HELEN: It depends.
SIMON: You're so right. Anyway, let's change the subject. [*Pause.*] About Mal's car. It's a new Valiant. White with wire wheels.
HELEN: Is that something special?
SIMON: Not really. Mal thinks it is. He's really excited. [*Pause.*] Listen, we're all going up to the hills for a grog-on tomorrow. Just to give the Valiant a try-out. Like to come?
HELEN: I've something else on tomorrow.
SIMON: Oh well, some other time. [*Pause.*] Hey, sorry. I haven't asked you your name.

HELEN: Helen.
SIMON: Pleased to meet you, Helen. You must come down and meet the boys some time. We have a lot of fun. I'm sure you'll like them once you get to know them. They're real individuals. You'll never have met anybody like them. I'll call up and nab you sometime over the weekend. What do you drink?
HELEN: Beer.
SIMON: Beauty. The same here. How about Saturday evening after we all come back from the hills? I'll call up as soon as we get back.
HELEN: Sorry, I won't be in until late.
SIMON: How about Sunday?
HELEN: I could be in.

SIMON: Terrific. [*Pause.*] What do you do for a crust?
HELEN: Oh, I've had all sorts of jobs.
SIMON: A woman of many roles, eh?

> *She nods.*

Doing anything at the moment?
HELEN: Just waiting.
SIMON: Getting the lie of the land?
HELEN: [*smiling*] Something like that.
SIMON: Where were you before this?
HELEN: [*looking around*] Excuse me. There's my taxi.
SIMON: [*standing and peering*] Hey, a new Rover too!

> HELEN *stands.*

You're doing it in style. Oh, you're off. [*Following her*] Marvellous to have met you. Don't forget to be around on Sunday!
HELEN: [*disappearing*] I won't. 'Bye!
SIMON: [*eyeing her off as she walks away offstage*] See you!

> *He stands musing for a while then walks across to the counter and deposits his milkshake container.*

Thanks, Alf.

> SIMON *exits, whistling.*

VOICE: Thanks, Rod, I mean, Mal.

> *The hairy arm appears through the aperture, gropes around, then takes the container. Pause. A plume of smoke is blown out through the aperture, preceded by a loud belch. Pause.*

Sorry.

SCENE SEVEN

Evening. A table and chairs.

ROD, MAL *and* SIMON *enter noisily with shouts and laughter. They are all drunk.* MAL *carries half a dozen bottles in a bag.*

ROD: Put 'em in the fridge, Digger!
MAL: No! Let's crack 'em now.
ROD: The others'll be colder. Drag 'em out. They must be chilled.
MAL: Right, chief.

>ROD *and* SIMON *collapse into chairs as* MAL *leaves.*

SIMON: Hey, that was marvellous up there this afternoon. Not too many people and pleasant surroundings. Not too many people. That's very important. Gives the place a touch of class. Don't you think so, Rod?

>ROD *belches.*

Was that yes or no?

>ROD *belches again and combines it with a 'yes'.*

What a comedian! [*He roars laughing.*] Too much.

>MAL *enters with beer and glasses.*

I was just saying to Rod what a beaut place that pub up in the hills is. We must go there more often. A real little paradise. Kookaburras, lyrebirds, bellbirds, a jukebox and friendly service.

>MAL *is pouring out the beer.*

Stick to it, Mal! More friendly service.
ROD: You're right. We must hit it more often. The Universal Joint is becoming far too popular.

They all drink.

SIMON: Ahhh. A nice drop.
ROD: Jesus, it's two hours since we've had a beer.
MAL: Well, you would want to go to that posh Chinese restaurant. The food was hardly worth the hour's wait. And that Chinese tea! Tasted like diluted piss.
ROD: Now how would you know what diluted piss tasted like?
MAL: I had it tonight.
ROD: Well, I happen to know that they use genuine Chinese tea at that place. I once went there with an Asian, and he said so.
MAL: Haven't we all been to a Chinese cafe with an Asian and been told

this? It's obvious they turn it on for their mates. Wake up.

ROD: Anyway, I say the food was worth it.

MAL: I would've preferred a dozen dim-sims from around the corner and a couple of extra bottles. [*Pause.*] Hey, Simon! Snap out of it! How about scaling those stairs and seeing if this new girl is in? You've been talking about her all day. I want to see if she is as good as you say she is. Come on. No stalling, deliver us the goods.

SIMON: [*annoyed*] Go and see for yourself.

MAL: No. I couldn't do that. Don't even know the girl. You're the one that has conned the girl, or so you tell us. Leap up those stairs, lover-boy, and haul her down for our expert perusal.

SIMON: I've already explained to you that she won't be home until late tonight.

ROD: How early's late?

MAL: Or how late's early for you, Simon, old cock?

SIMON: What time is it now?

MAL: Nearly ten o'clock.

ROD: That's pretty late, you know.

MAL: Very late for a young girl in a strange area.

ROD: Yes, where does she come from?

SIMON: I didn't ask her.

MAL: Ha! You didn't get very far.

SIMON: I got far enough to find out what her movements were over the weekend.

MAL: Big deal.

SIMON: At least I've seen the girl.

MAL: Ugly as sin.

ROD: Face like a warped sandshoe.

They laugh. The glasses are filled up.

SIMON: Just wait.

ROD: We're waiting. Why don't you just slip up and see if she's in?

MAL: No harm in that.

ROD: Don't tell me a smoothie like you is frightened!

MAL: I refuse to believe it.

ROD: [*gloating*] I think I may be right.

MAL: You gutless wonder!

SIMON: Don't be bloody stupid. Of course it's not true. I don't see much point in going up when she said she wouldn't be back until late. Late means midnight or so. Too late to call up anyway.

MAL: [*in a sing-song voice*] Simon's piking out.

ROD: Yellow belly.

MAL: Come on, Simon, sock down that glass and I'll recharge it for you. Another to gather up courage. Herb over that bottle, will you, Rod?

> ROD *passes him a bottle. He opens it and fills up* SIMON's *glass.*

Atta boy, Simon.

ROD: Drink it down, Simon.

SIMON: Why don't you all go to hell?!

MAL: Now, now. Don't get excited. [*To* ROD] This woman must really be something if Simon is stalling like this. Must really be something.

ROD: Beautiful and for*mid*able, eh?

SIMON: She's beautiful, that's for sure. I didn't find her so *form*idable.

ROD: Don't believe it.

SIMON: Believe what you like. She's just another good-looking woman. They're everywhere. Three a penny. All around us.

MAL: [*stretching his arms above his head*] All around us?

ROD: [*with a dismissive gesture towards the auditorium*] The place is full of them.

MAL: Crawling with them.

ROD: Pity they're not here.

MAL: [*shaking his head in despair*] Yes, pity we can't see them.

ROD: It's so lonely.

> ROD *and* MAL *laugh.* SIMON *looks sour. Pause.*

Hey, I thought I heard someone go upstairs.

> *Pause. They listen.*

Yes, I heard the door go very faintly. The flat above. Here's your big chance, Simon.

MAL: No choice now, Simon.

SIMON: Right, I'm on my way.

ROD: The man of the moment!

> SIMON *rises, finishes off his beer, and exits.*

MAL: We'll soon see.

ROD: Wonder how long he'll take?

MAL: It'll be open rivalry if she's a doll. We're all on the loose now.

ROD: Just don't cramp my style.

MAL: What a joke.

ROD: It's no joke. I can be very nasty when aroused.

MAL: Like a bull in a china shop. I'm terrified. Look, my hands are trembling.

MAL *extends his hands. They shake, more like a genuine tremble than a faked one.*

ROD: Hey, you really are shaking.

MAL: Bulldust!

ROD: Is this going to be easy?! It's going to be a one-man race. No worries at all.

MAL: Don't put too many tickets on yourself. I'm by no means out of the…

> SIMON *and* HELEN *enter.*

SIMON: Well, here we are, Helen.

> MAL *and* ROD *stand.*

Helen, meet Mal, and Rod.

HELEN: How do you do?

MAL & ROD: [*together*] Glad to meet you, Helen.

> MAL *and* ROD *look at each other knowingly.*

SIMON: I'll fetch you a chair, Helen.

> SIMON *walks out.*

MAL: Have mine, Helen.

HELEN: [*sitting down*] Thank you.

MAL: Simon is now fetching his own chair.

> MAL *and* ROD *laugh, then both sit down.* SIMON *returns with a chair and a glass.*

SIMON: Could you use a beer, Helen?

HELEN: Yes, I will have one.

> *Pause.* SIMON *pours her a beer.*

MAL: Like a drop, do you?

HELEN: [*smiling*] Yes. [*Taking the beer from* SIMON] Thank you.

ROD: That's the way. Then you're not out of things.

MAL: No danger of that around here.

> SIMON *hauls a fresh bottle out of a pocket, opens it, and fills up the glasses.*

SIMON: Well, here's to Helen, the new girl.

SIMON, ROD & MAL: [*together*] Cheers!

> *They all drink. Pause.*

ROD: How do you like your new flat?

HELEN: Oh, it's not too bad. A little small, but it will have to do for the time being.

SIMON: You're not thinking of shifting camp?
HELEN: No.
SIMON: You had me worried. Thought we were just going to get to know you and then lose you.

She shakes her head.

MAL: Beaut. We like a bit of female company.
HELEN: It's good to know you're welcome.
MAL: Welcome! That's an understatement. Relax. Feel at home. We're an easy-going gang.
ROD: Easy come, easy go.

The three men drink. Pause.

Do you know what we did today?
HELEN: No.
ROD: We all zorched up to a pub in the hills in Mal's new Valiant. A great day.
SIMON: That's why we're all a bit primed.
HELEN: I see. What does—?
ROD: The car went really well, don't you think, Mal?
MAL: Not too bad, considering I couldn't fully extend her.
SIMON: But you went over the limit a few times.
MAL: Not by much. That was mainly to test the acceleration on the hills.
SIMON: She's got plenty of toes in that department.
ROD: No worries there.
SIMON: What did the fuel consumption come out to again?
MAL: About twenty-eight to the gallon.
ROD: That's pretty good.
MAL: [*very pleased*] Yes.
SIMON: More than I would've expected.
MAL: Still, it will be lower in the suburbs. All the stopping and starting.
SIMON: Still, you can't expect much better from a big car.
ROD: It's not that big.
SIMON: Well, it's bigger than the average family car.
ROD: True.

HELEN *is obviously left out of things.*

MAL: What did you think of the white duco and wire wheels once you saw them, Simon?
SIMON: I was won over. Really looks good, Mal. I was wrong there.
MAL: That's one to remember. Simon admits he was wrong.

SIMON: Cut it out. I'm open to reason.
ROD: Yes, defend yourself in the face of this slander, Simon.
MAL: More beer, chaps. Helen?

> HELEN *holds out her glass.* MAL *fills it up and then pours all round.*

Must go and get another Aristotle.

> *He walks out.*

ROD: Did you notice that rattle under the back of the car on the way back? Only faint.
SIMON: Yes, I did.
ROD: Seemed pretty serious to me. Rear transmission.
SIMON: Bulldust! Probably a loose exhaust pipe.
ROD: You think so?

> MAL *returns with a bottle.*

SIMON: [*to* MAL] Rod thinks that rattle under the back was the rear transmission.
MAL: He obviously doesn't know what he's talking about. Just a loose exhaust pipe. Didn't think it worth mentioning.
ROD: Perhaps you were too worried about it.
MAL: Don't be a moron.
ROD: Well, my old Vanguard once had a rattle like that. People kept telling me it was the exhaust pipe. It became louder and louder, until I had it seen to. Rear transmission. Cost me thirty bloody notes. Now I'd have that seen to, Mal.
MAL: Your ignorance of cars, Rod, is legendary. So we won't pursue the subject any further.
ROD: Well, don't say I didn't tell you.
MAL: I won't have to.
SIMON: [*winking at* ROD] Well, Ace wasn't very impressed with the car.
MAL: We all know Ace dislikes any car that even looks vaguely American, or rather anything that is not made on the Continent. He won't settle for anything less than a Ferrari.
ROD: Still, he knows what he is talking about when it comes to cars, any sort of car.
MAL: But he's prejudiced about cars of American design.

> *Pause.*

SIMON: What do you think of the steering?
MAL: That will need a little adjustment. It's only a minor thing. There are bound to be small problems cropping up. It's only natural. Teething

troubles.

ROD: Do you call a buggered rear transmission teething troubles?

MAL: Don't you ever give up?

ROD: I've got a feeling about that rattle. It's a death rattle.

MAL: Well, forget about it, for Christ's sake! The exhaust pipe will be tightened on Monday. Overall, I'm very happy with it, in spite of your doubts and the sneering of Ace O'Hanlon.

SIMON: Anyway, Mal. I think you've got a good car. [*Pause.*] But just wait until I've got my Rover!

MAL: If you get it.

SIMON: I will. Regardless of your boss. Now there's a real car, and not exactly a poor performer.

MAL: Don't talk crap! It's just a good solid reliable car. Just have a geek at the figures. It doesn't compare with the Valiant.

ROD: Good point. Look at the figures.

SIMON: Crap!

MAL: Get a grip of yourself, Simon. Are you seriously going to compare a '62 Rover with the latest Valiant? It's not in the bloody race! Anything you like to name. Take spare parts in a Rover, for instance. They're incredibly expensive!

SIMON: But you rarely need spare parts in a Rover.

ROD: The figures are the important thing.

MAL: Yes! Just look at the figures. They're as plain as your face. You just can't close your eyes to them.

SIMON: Seeing is believing?

MAL: Of course.

ROD: The umpire's decision is final.

MAL: The odds are against you, Simon.

SIMON: It's all right in theory, but what about in practice?

MAL: When the chips are down, the Rover doesn't carry any weight.

> HELEN *stands.*

ROD: Knock it off, you two. You both can't see the wood for the trees. Just wait until I get my new Ford Mustang. That'll be a real eye-opener.

MAL & SIMON: [*together*] Your what?!

> HELEN *leaves unnoticed.*

ROD: My new Mustang, chaps.

MAL: What bulldust!

SIMON: I've heard the lot.

ROD: It's a fact, men.

MAL: Since when?
ROD: Since I got my last raise in pay. Should be able to trade the old job in soon. Got my eyes on a red one, rooster red. A beautiful little unit.
MAL: Hit me, but don't shit me!
SIMON: How pretentious can you get?!
ROD: It's no more pretentious than you buying a Rover, or Mal a white Valiant with wire wheels.
SIMON: Oh, yes it is.
MAL: That's for sure.
ROD: [*laughing*] You're both jealous!

MAL: [*leaping up*] Of a flashy Mustang?!
SIMON: Not likely.
ROD: [*standing*] What about its bloody tremendous performance?!
MAL: I haven't seen the figures.
ROD: Its top speed is around a hundred and twenty.
MAL: You won't get me in it with you at that speed.
SIMON: Me neither.
ROD: I wouldn't ask you.
SIMON: [*leaping up*] If you ever get a Mustang!
ROD: I will!
MAL: [*shouting*] Crap!
SIMON: [*shouting*] Bulldust!
ROD: [*shouting*] I'll piss on the lot of you!
MAL: Crap!
SIMON: Bulldust!

> *The sounds of racing cars in action are heard, at first soft, but increasing in volume as the argument becomes more absurd.*

ROD: I'll thrash the arse off you both!
MAL: You couldn't drive a tack!
ROD: I'd drive you into the ground!
MAL: Crap!
SIMON: Not in a Mustang!
MAL: Valiant!
ROD: Mustang!
SIMON: Rover!

> *The argument descends further into a shouting match with pushes and shoves as well as gesticulations. Names like Bugatti, Stutz and Stanley Steamer become prominent. The absurdity of the argument and its snowballing quality should be heightened by full technical*

effects—flashing lights, colours, silhouette or shadow lighting, etc. The argument is finally swamped by the racing car sounds at extremely loud volume and these lead to a climactic chorus of car horns, klaxons, even foghorns perhaps. Suddenly there is darkness and silence. This leads immediately into Scene Eight.

SCENE EIGHT

Darkness.

HELEN *is revealed downstage to one side.*

HELEN: The purpose of this play,
Should the playwright have his way,
Is general and not particular,
For Malcolm, Rod and Simon are
Not simply the blacker side of white.
Please flip the coin tonight.

> *Pause. A knocking is heard.* HELEN *doesn't seem to hear it. Pause. More knocking is heard, louder.*

Come in!

> MAL *enters. He carries two car wheels, one is a wire wheel, the other a hubcap type.*

MAL: It's me, Mal.
HELEN: Yes.
MAL: [*standing beside* HELEN *in the light*] Excuse me, Helen, but I thought you'd be interested.
HELEN: What?
MAL: Well, in these. I brought you these two wheels to have a look at.
HELEN: Thank you.
MAL: Do you like them?
HELEN: Very much.
MAL: Which do you prefer?
HELEN: I don't know. They all have their advantages.
MAL: Some people, especially my friends, think the wire wheel is too flash. Do you agree?
HELEN: It depends.
MAL: Exactly. I'm glad you agree, Helen. Really glad. You've been a great help. It's terribly important to me Helen, that you agree. It's been getting me down. Lots of things have been troubling me lately. Colours, especially. I have nightmares about colours. Terrible colours. Colours that do things to me. Reds that actually burn and scorch, whites that freeze, greys that smother, greens that smell and slide like slime, yellows that drain me of all energy, make me weak and faint. And colours I've never see before, and never want to mention. And

black, a thick and powerful colour that unsexes me. [*Pause.*] Which colour do you like?

HELEN: All of them.

MAL: Is white right?

HELEN: White is right.

MAL: You've been a great help to me. You've no idea, no idea at all. [*Pause.*] It's a windy night. Cold, wet and windy. [*Pause.*] Could I stay the night here?

HELEN: No.

MAL: Please.

HELEN: No.

MAL: Why not? [*Pause. Silence.*] Just this one night. I won't do anything. I promise. I just want to lie there. I won't bother you ever again.

HELEN: No.

MAL: I have to go?

HELEN: Yes.

MAL: Out into the black. [*Pause.*] Goodnight. [*Walking across the stage with the two wheels*]
My head is not exactly clear,
I don't know what I'm doing,
My dreams are thick with fear,
I'm frightened
And unenlightened,
I think there's something brewing.

He exits. Pause. A knock is heard.

HELEN: Come in!

SIMON *enters carrying a steering wheel.*

SIMON: [*approaching her*] Excuse me for disturbing you, Helen; it's me, Simon.

HELEN: Oh, it's you.

SIMON: Yes, it's me. I brought this steering wheel along. What do you think of it?

HELEN: It's a fine steering wheel.

SIMON: It is, indeed. I'm so glad you agree. I just wanted you to agree. Nothing more than that. A lot of people, especially my friends, don't like this sort of steering wheel. But I think it has a real touch of class, truly round with well-designed finger-grips, something you can really hang on to. I have nightmares about things slipping away from me, not being able to hang on, slipping down ice-smooth slopes, blood-red slopes, but smooth and slippery. At other times I'm climbing a long ladder in the middle of nowhere. And for every rung I climb the ladder moves down one. I never get any further up that ladder in spite of all my efforts. It's a terrible feeling of marking time. And up on that ladder the temperature of the wind doesn't change. Why is that?

HELEN: You have no sail.

SIMON: But I'm buying a '62 Rover. What do you think of that?

HELEN: Nothing.

SIMON: I'm glad you agree. It's necessary to agree on some things. It really helps. [*Pause.*] The streets are wet and slippery. Too much rain for winter. [*Pause.*] Can I stay here with you?

HELEN: No.

SIMON: I won't do anything. I'll just sit and watch you. Perhaps grip your hand.

HELEN: No.

SIMON: What do I do?

HELEN: Walk with the wind, Simon Peter.

Pause.

SIMON: [*walking across the stage with the steering wheel*]
My head is not exactly clear,
I don't know what I'm doing,
My dreams are thick with fear,
I'm frightened
And unenlightened,
I think there's something brewing.

He exits. Pause. A knock is heard.

HELEN: Come in!

ROD *enters with a gearstick and gearbox (floor change).*

ROD: [*approaching* HELEN] Excuse me, Helen, for interrupting. I brought you this. [*Pause.*] It's me, Rod. [*Pause.*] What do you think of it? It has a very smooth action. [*Demonstrating*] Click, click, click. Synchro-mesh in all gears. Straight from top to first. Reverse is very simple. A beautiful piece of work. What I've always wanted in a gearbox. What do you think?

HELEN: It's a work of art.

ROD: I'm glad you like it, Helen. Thanks. A lot of people, especially my friends, don't approve. I think it's important to have the right sort of gearbox. It's part of your life. You can kill people if you don't have the right sort of gearbox. And that's the last thing I want to do. Kill people. I couldn't live with myself if I killed someone through something silly like that. I have these terrible dreams about killing people. Cold-blooded, malicious murder with my own hands. I walk up to them and coldly tell them that I am going to kill them. I do it. With a screwdriver, a grease gun, or my own grease-stained fingers. Throttle them. They are invariably helpless old women who are strangely strong and defiant in their death. No hysterics or begging, just a look of calm collected knowledge. They know, and I am rejected before I do it. As they die they grow younger and younger. It's always then that I run, never stay, but run into the next victim. There's always another one before me. Why do I murder people in my dreams?

HELEN: Because you've never been murdered.

ROD: Just wait until I get my new Mustang. [*Pause.*] Can I stay the night with you?

HELEN: No.

ROD: Just tonight. I won't bother you again.

HELEN: No.

ROD: I won't do anything. I'd be happy just to sit in the corner and watch you sleep.

Pause.

HELEN: Goodnight.

ROD: Goodnight. [*Walking across the stage with the gearstick and gearbox*]
My head is not exactly clear,
I don't know what I'm doing,
My dreams are thick with fear,
I'm frightened
And unenlightened,
I think there's something brewing.

> *He exits. Darkness and music, preferably early 'Beach Boys'. A tableau is suddenly revealed. It is composed of ROD, MAL and SIMON supporting the wheels, steering wheel, gearstick, etc. in the form of a car, and huddling together as if in a car and driving at high speed. There is no movement whatsoever. The music is in the background now. The lighting illuminating the tableau should be garish and eerie—a green, for example. The scene is held for some 15 to 30 seconds. Darkness.*

SCENE NINE

Table and chairs. Evening.

MAL *sits at the table reading a newspaper. He drinks milk straight from a pint bottle.*

MAL: Bugger-all in the news tonight. [*He gurgles down more milk.*] Not even a good-looking sort.

   A knock is heard.

Yeah!

   HELEN *enters.*

Why, hello!

HELEN: Hello, Mal.

MAL: Have a seat. How are things?

HELEN: Good. I just called in to thank you for the other night.

MAL: No trouble at all. A pleasure. Did you enjoy yourself?

HELEN: Yes.

MAL: Beauty. We're a wild lot. I seem to remember we argued all night.

HELEN: That's right.

MAL: That's the beauty of living with other blokes. Always something to discuss and thrash out. No end to it. [*Pause.*] Like a swig at the milk?

HELEN: No thanks.

MAL: Prefer the stronger stuff?

HELEN: Always.

MAL: Excuse me, then, while I down the rest of this bottle.

   He drains it.

HELEN: What a man.

MAL: Sure you wouldn't like a bash at some?

HELEN: Not just at the moment.

MAL: One of the great fluids. Milk. Puts hair on your chest.

HELEN: And lead in your pencil.

   MAL *is taken aback by this, even shocked. Pause.*

MAL: Er, what are you doing this week?

HELEN: Nothing much.

MAL: Would you like to come out with me one night this week?

HELEN: Love to.

MAL: Beauty. Name the night then. I'm easy.

HELEN: Tomorrow night?

MAL: Tremendous. It's a date. [*Pause.*] Where would you like to go?

   She shrugs her shoulders.

Well, I had a musical in mind.

HELEN: What's it called?

MAL: 'The Trial'.
HELEN: What on earth is it about?
MAL: A trial I suppose.
HELEN: Go on. Doesn't seem a very suitable subject for a musical.
MAL: No doubt there'll be briefs everywhere. [*He laughs uproariously at his own pun.*] Not bad, eh? [*Pause.*] Well, it's advertised everywhere. That's good enough for me. [*Pause.*] It's amazing what they can put to music these days. It all started with the '1812 Overture'.
HELEN: What did?
MAL: The musical, of course. [*Pause.*] I'll call up about seven.
HELEN: I should've girded my loins by then.

    SIMON *enters.*

SIMON: Hello there. What a surprise.
MAL: [*gesturing to* HELEN] Called in to see us.
SIMON: [*sitting down*] Terrific. Do it more often. [*He looks at the empty milk bottle. To* MAL] Suppose you've sunk all the milk?
MAL: [*peeved*] No. [*Pause.*] Simon is very touchy about his milk, you know.
HELEN: [*to* SIMON] Were you breast-fed?
SIMON: Was I what?
MAL: [*laughing*] Breast-fed.
SIMON: [*blushing*] I wouldn't know.
HELEN: [*to* MAL] Were you?
MAL: Sure to have been. My mother had a pair of whoppers.

    HELEN *and* MAL *laugh.*

SIMON: [*to* MAL] That's a bit rough!
MAL: [*pulling himself together*] Sorry, Helen.

    The phone is heard ringing.

I'll answer it.

    MAL *leaves.*

HELEN: [*amused*] Whether or not you are breast-fed has nothing to do with the size of your mother's norks. How mad can you get?
SIMON: [*uneasily*] Yes. If that were true, Asian babies would hardly crack it for a feed. It's common knowledge that Asian birds are flat-chested.
HELEN: They have other anatomical deformities as well.
SIMON: [*acutely embarrassed*] Er, yes. Well, I… all right…
HELEN: [*laughing*] Horizontal—
MAL: [*as he enters; excitedly*] Hey! You'll never guess what Ronnie has

gone and done!
SIMON: [*relieved*] What?
HELEN: Sweet Fanny Adams.
MAL: He's gone and bought a new Alfa!
SIMON: The bastard! Excuse me, Helen.
HELEN: The bastard!
SIMON: Why didn't he tell us before?
HELEN: The bastard.
MAL: Just to spring it on us. Bit hard to take.
HELEN: The bastard.
SIMON: He's such a crappy driver.
MAL: Too much. Ronnie in an Alfa.
HELEN: Does she have a horizontal or a vertical take-off?
MAL: [*amazed*] What?
HELEN: [*playing it dumb*] Alfa.
MAL: It's a car!
SIMON: Don't play the fool, Helen.
MAL: Think I'll flash over and see it. Coming?
SIMON: Er, no.
MAL: Come on. Show Ronnie your cornering technique. He could do with a few more clues.
SIMON: Later. I'll see it next time he's around.
MAL: Well, I'm off. Can't wait. See you both.
SIMON: So long.

> HELEN *gives* MAL *a big wave as he leaves.*

Are you all right?
HELEN: Fantastic.

> *Pause.*

SIMON: What are you up to this week?
HELEN: Nothing much.
SIMON: Would you like to come out one night this week?
HELEN: Love to.
SIMON: What night suits you?
HELEN: Tomorrow night.
SIMON: Beauty. [*Pause.*] Any clues as to where?
HELEN: Apparently there's a new musical in town called 'The Trial'. It's about the problems encountered by a lady solicitor in the pursuit of her profession. Riddled with legal wit.
SIMON: Sounds very interesting. I'll call up 'round seven tomorrow.

ROD *enters.*

ROD: Hello there, everybody! How are you, Helen?

HELEN: Fine. And you?

ROD: Great. Never been in better form. I feel really dangerous tonight.

SIMON: Think I'll try that milk.

SIMON leaves. ROD *sits down. Pause.*

ROD: Well, Helen, how is the world treating you?

HELEN: It's a bit trying at times.

ROD: How come?

HELEN: Trivial things, really.

ROD: You shouldn't let the trifles get you down. Look at me, a ball of muscle. The secret is not letting *anything* get you down. You probably take things too seriously.

Pause. HELEN *smiles.*

HELEN: Anyway, I'm in a beaut mood tonight.

ROD: Really happy?

HELEN: Really happy.

ROD: Glad to hear it.

SIMON *returns.*

SIMON: That milk was right off! I'll king-hit that Mal when I see him.

ROD: You do that.

SIMON: Hey, did you know that Ronnie's gone and bought a new Alfa?

ROD: No.

SIMON: Too much.

ROD: Too much.

HELEN: Too much.

SIMON: Bit of a joke, eh? He's such a crappy driver.

ROD: A work of art like that is wasted on Ronnie.

SIMON: Mal's flashed off to see it. [*Pause. Awkwardly*] Think I'll dash down to the milk bar and sock away a pint or so before I head off to the office. Got a lot to catch up on. See you.

SIMON *exits.*

ROD: You'll get on!

HELEN: Ciao!

ROD: That boy really knows what he's about. There'll be no stopping him in that firm. Be a director in a few years.

HELEN: And you?

ROD: No. I'm making slow but steady progress. Not in Simon's class. He's a

fanatic. Lives for the firm. Like a beer?
HELEN: No thanks. [*Pause.*] Were you breast-fed?

ROD: Was I what?
HELEN: [*moving closer to him*] Were you breast-fed?
ROD: [*taken aback*] I, er… wouldn't know.
HELEN: [*closer*] Did your mother have a good pair?
ROD: Eh?
HELEN: Was she an Asian?
ROD: [*retreating*] Er, no, I—
HELEN: You can tell, you know.
ROD: [*standing and backing away*] Sure you wouldn't like a beer?
HELEN: [*staring pointedly*] It's very, very easy.
ROD: [*sheepish; against the wall*] What is?
HELEN: To tell.
ROD: What is?

> HELEN *laughs.* ROD, *confused for a few seconds, eventually returns to the table and sits. Pause.*

Don't think I, er, really want one either, you know. Got a bucks' turn on tonight. One of my old schoolmates is signing his life away. Could be a wild ding. They've hired a striptease girl for the occasion. What a knockout. Fingers Phelan is going to accompany her on the bongos. Crazy. Anyway, I'd better not start now or they'll be carrying me home as well as the poor prick in whose aid the function is being held. Don't want to lose my concentration too early just in case this strip woman turns out to be a winner. [*Pause.*] What are you up to this week?
HELEN: Nothing particularly major.
ROD: How'd you like to take in a show with me?
HELEN: How could I resist?
ROD: What night suits you? I'm free all week.
HELEN: Tomorrow night would be perfect.
ROD: Beauty. [*Pause.*] Anywhere in particular you'd like to go?
HELEN: Yes. A new musical called 'The Trial'.
ROD: I've heard good reports about that.
HELEN: It's supposed to be the first really sad musical.
ROD: I could do with a good solid weep. Pick you up about seven, right?
HELEN: Right. [*Pause.*] Well, I must be off.

> *She stands.*

ROD: So soon?

HELEN: Yes. Anyway, you've a big night ahead of you.
ROD: True.

Pause. She turns to go.

You wouldn't like a milkshake?
HELEN: Not just at the moment, thanks.
ROD: [*standing*] Think I will. Settles the stomach. Gives it lining, you know.

HELEN *exits.*

[*Walking after her*] It'll need one. [*Standing*] Boy, am going to write myself off tonight!

SCENE TEN

Same scene.

SIMON *enters, whistling. He wears a smart suit, and stands adjusting his tie and attending to his hair.* MAL *enters. He also is in a cheerful mood, and like* SIMON, *is dressed in a snappy suit. He carries a bunch of flowers.*

SIMON: This looks promising. Off on the tear tonight?
MAL: That's right. Have to be in top form tonight. Like the flowers?
SIMON: Beautiful. Pity you haven't got a bigger bunch. I could use some.
MAL: Are you heading out too?
SIMON: Obviously. Can't you tell? [*He holds out his arms and turns around.*] Smart, eh?
MAL: Too smart. Almost international. Who are you racing off?
SIMON: Have a guess.
MAL: Cath?
SIMON: No. [*Firmly*] I told you I'd finished with her. I mean what I say.
MAL: Not always. You've been known to back down before this. Come on, who is it?
SIMON: Helen, from upstairs.
MAL: No bulldust. Who is she really? Who's the victim tonight?
SIMON: I'm telling you. It's Helen, the new girl.
MAL: Pull the other leg.
SIMON: I'm dead serious.
MAL: I hope not. I've got a date with her tonight.
SIMON: Ha, ha, ha.

MAL: [*sneeringly*] Ha, ha to you too. It's true.
SIMON: Since when?
MAL: I asked her last night.
SIMON: So did I.
MAL: Must be some mistake.
SIMON: She must have her dates mixed up.
MAL: Last night?
SIMON: She could've. She's a bit vague, you know.

> ROD *enters. He is sharply dressed in a suit and carries a box of chocolates. He is gay and whistling.*

ROD: [*breezily*] Hello there, chaps.
MAL & SIMON: [*together*] Hello.

> *Pause.* ROD *adjusts his tie. The other two stare at* ROD *and the chocolates.*

SIMON: Heading out tonight, Rod?
ROD: Am I what? Been a bit too classy for you blokes. Taking Helen out, from upstairs.
SIMON & MAL: [*together*] What?!
MAL: Knock it off.
ROD: Why, isn't that allowed?
MAL: The bitch!
SIMON: Screw me.
ROD: Please tell me if I'm stepping on anybody's toes.
SIMON: What the Christ is she up to?!
ROD: What's the big secret?
MAL: She's arranged to go out with all of us tonight.
ROD: [*incredulously*] Oh, yes.
SIMON: It's true.
MAL: Too bloody true.
ROD: It better not be.
SIMON: I asked her out last night.
MAL: So did I.
ROD: So did I.
SIMON: That makes three of us.
ROD: She's lined us all up!
MAL: You said it.
ROD: What a bitch! Who does she think she is?
MAL: I think we'd better go right up there and find out what's going on.
SIMON: Mmm.
ROD: Could be a bit embarrassing for us.

SIMON: For her. What if she's made a genuine mistake?
ROD: What bloody rot. She's having us on. *Smart* bitch.
MAL: Why don't we draw from a pack of cards? Lowest card wins her.
ROD: Bugger that.
MAL: Well, I think I asked her out first.
MAL: You can't pull that one on us. Anyway, do you really want to take her out now? Have some pride.
SIMON: Well, what do we do?

> *Pause.*

ROD: I know. We systematically embarrass her.
MAL: How?
ROD: We take it in turns to go up and collect her. Each a few minutes apart.
MAL: Take me more than a few minutes to bowl her over.
ROD: She won't know where she is.
SIMON: It won't work. I know. We'll be more embarrassed than she will be. She has *us* set up. What I can't work out is why she would want to do it. She can't have anything against us.
ROD: She's a natural bitch. Treating us like puppets, or pawns.
SIMON: What do we do?
MAL: Stuffed if I know.
ROD: I'll think of something. Can't let her get away with this.

> *Pause. A knock is heard.*

SIMON: [*abruptly*] Come in!

> HELEN *enters. She looks calmly around.* SIMON, ROD *and* MAL *exchange looks of dismay and confusion.*

Er, hello, Helen!
MAL: [*to* HELEN] What's going on?

> *She ignores him and signals to* SIMON *with a vague smile.*

HELEN: Could I see you for a moment, Simon?
SIMON: [*weakly*] Er, sure, Helen.

> *Highly embarrassed,* SIMON *looks at* MAL *and* ROD *in turn, then follows* HELEN *out. Pause.*

ROD: Christ.
MAL: Root my boot and shag my shoe.
ROD: What next?
MAL: She seems to know what she is up to.
ROD: I bloody well hope so. Because I don't.
MAL: What happens now?

ROD: How the hell would I know?!
MAL: All right, don't get excited.

Pause. They sit down.

I suggest a few rapid cans.
ROD: You would.

Pause.

MAL: She must be going to apologise to us separately. [*Pause.*] What a pack of Arabs we must have looked, all dressed up and clutching gifts.
ROD: She better have a good explanation.
MAL: She didn't look at all guilty.
ROD: You're right.
MAL: *She* should've looked guilty, not us.
ROD: The bitch is trying to put one over us.

Pause.

MAL: Where were you going to take her?
ROD: In her room, where else?
MAL: Funny. Where were you heading out?
ROD: To that musical, 'The Trial'.
MAL: Hey, so was I. She suggested it.
ROD: Same here. An obvious set-up.
MAL: The two-timing tart.

From left: Edward Simpson as Mal, Ian Drysdale as Simon, Steve Vella as Rod and Melissa Docker as Helen in the 1997 London Arts Theatre Club production.

ROD: She can cough up for all the seats we bought.
MAL: Stuff and corruption, I'd forgotten about that.
ROD: Too late for refunds.
MAL: She has to follow it through now. [*Pause.*] No pulling out now. One of us will dip his wick before the night's out.
ROD: You hope.
MAL: I always hope for that.

    Pause.

ROD: Serve her right.
MAL: It's a pointless trick really.
ROD: She probably thinks she's some sort of comedian.
MAL: Why take it out on us? [*Pause.*] She must have a jaundiced outlook on life.
ROD: She's warped. It's as simple as that.
MAL: Someone's done something to her along the line. There must be some explanation.
ROD: It'd better be bloody good.
MAL: Let's wait and see what Simon has to say.
ROD: If he comes back.
MAL: He wouldn't do the dirty on us.
ROD: I don't trust anyone in a situation like this. Every man for himself.
MAL: Even friends?
ROD: Friends especially.
MAL: Nice type.
ROD: Friends make the best enemies.
MAL: By Christ, if he races her off, it'll be the last fat he cracks.
ROD: Shut up.

    Long pause. Silence.

I wonder what's going on up there.
MAL: It's strangely quiet.

    They both stare at the ceiling and listen. Pause. They continue to throw glances up at the ceiling over the next few minutes.

ROD: Can't hear any raised voices.

    Long pause. They fidget and listen.

MAL: Shhh! [*Pause.*] Thought I heard Simon laughing. Very eerie.
ROD: You're imagining things.

    ROD *lights a cigarette. Pause.*

MAL: That's odd.

ROD: [*impatiently*] What?

MAL: Positive I heard someone sobbing.

ROD: I can't hear a bloody thing. You're cracking up.

MAL: Probably Helen.

ROD: For sure. [*Pause.*] Jesus! Nothing annoys me more than bugger-ups like this!

MAL: Everything was going so smoothly too.

ROD: [*cynically*] For all of us.

MAL: Well, for me.

ROD: Crap. We were all in the same position.

MAL: I suppose so.

ROD: Still got tickets on yourself?

MAL: A forest of them. [*Pause.*] It could've been marvellous. A handy knock upstairs for one of us. A real doll too. It would have to happen like this.

ROD: [*cynically*] A real doll.

MAL: Still, I suppose there's hope for one of us.

ROD: It's all over bar the shouting as far as I'm concerned.

MAL: This could turn out to be quite humorous at a future date.

ROD: Not for me, mate. I don't like being played around with like this.

MAL: Anyway, there are plenty more where she came from.

Pause. A knock is heard.

Come in.

HELEN *enters.*

HELEN: Could I see you for a moment, Mal?

MAL: All right.

He follows her out. Pause. ROD *sits and smokes.*

ROD: Lucky last, I suppose. [*Pause.*] I wonder where Simon is? Not up there I hope.

Pause. He listens. He dashes his cigarette to the floor, stands on it and walks out. Pause. He returns with a can of beer, a glass and a magazine. He pours himself a beer and sits reading.

[*Throwing down the magazine*] Poop on this for a joke! No bitch is going to make a monkey out of me. [*Pause.*] Where the shagging hell is Simon?!

He stands and walks upstage, listening for sounds from upstairs. His beer is left untouched. Pause. SIMON *enters quietly and stands away from* ROD *downstage. Pause.*

[*Finally noticing* SIMON] Where have you been?
SIMON: Where would you reckon?
ROD: What happened? What did she say?
SIMON: [*shrugging his shoulders*] Nothing much.
ROD: [*approaching* SIMON; *angrily*] Stop stalling! What did she say?
SIMON: [*avoiding him*] I went and had a milkshake.
ROD: Didn't you go up to her room?
SIMON: Yes! Then I went 'round and had a milkshake. That bastard in the milk bar has put up the price of his milkshakes. By a cent.
ROD: [*grabbing* SIMON] Stop changing the subject, will you?! What happened?
SIMON: [*struggling*] Leave go, will you?
ROD: [*releasing him*] Well, stop being a prize bastard.
SIMON: [*moving away from* ROD] I just don't feel like talking about it.
ROD: [*following*] Well, I do.
SIMON: Leave me alone!
ROD: I've a good mind to slam you one.
SIMON: Try it.
ROD: Don't push me too far, Simon.
SIMON: Go flog yourself!
ROD: Do you really want to get snotted? It'd give me no end of pleasure to push that smug face of yours in.
SIMON: Smug? You ought to talk. You're the bastard that's always been smug and had tickets on himself. Not me. Especially with women, always playing the big operator.
ROD: [*grabbing* SIMON *again*] Now it's you.
SIMON: [*breaking free*] No. I just want to be left alone for while.
ROD: Poor, poor Simon. What did she do to you? Tell your Uncle Rod what that nasty girl did to you. Come to your mother, Simon, she knows what is best for you, she knows—

A knock is heard.

[*Aggressively*] Come in!

HELEN *enters.*

HELEN: Can you spare a moment, Rod?
ROD: Why? What do you want?
HELEN: It won't take long.
ROD: All right. It better not.

ROD *follows* HELEN *out. Pause.* SIMON *sits down. Pause.* MAL *enters. He joins* SIMON. *They sit in silence for some time, pretending to be occupied with trivial things, not wishing to speak.*

SIMON: Did you know that bastard at the milk bar has put up the price of milkshakes. By one cent.
MAL: No.
SIMON: Well, he has.
MAL: That's a bit rough. He only put them up a few months ago.
SIMON: We'll have to boycott the prick.
MAL: Just as well it's not beer or petrol. [*Pause.*] I was just thinking. The fuel consumption on the Valiant is not too bad around the suburbs. Not as bad as I thought it'd be. Not bad at all considering...
SIMON: Considering what?
MAL: Considering it's a big car.
SIMON: Not again! You're always saying that. Listen, you poor bastard, it's not such a big car. Anybody would think you were driving the latest Dodge or Daimler, not some jumped-up family car.
MAL: [*groaning*] Don't let's start this again.
SIMON: Well, you always bring it up with crap about the size of your Valiant. I have my gut crammed full of it.
MAL: So what?
SIMON: Can't you talk about anything else?
MAL: Why should I?
SIMON: Because it just isn't worth all the jaw-work, Jesus.
MAL: I suppose a Rover is.
SIMON: Can't you shut up?
MAL: I know. You're jealous.
SIMON: Crap.
MAL: [*victoriously*] You're bloody jealous! It's written all over your ugly dial.
SIMON: Of that?! You're obsessed by it. It's a very ordinary car, Malcolm dear.
MAL: You wouldn't know. Why don't you shut your mouth?!
SIMON: [*standing*] I've a good mind to punch you one.
MAL: [*laughing*] Try it.
SIMON: Don't push me too far.
MAL: [*standing*] Yawn.

> MAL *goes to turn away from* SIMON, *then suddenly lunges, pushing* SIMON *to the floor. He punches* SIMON *as he stands up.*

SIMON: [*winded*] You bastard.

> MAL *hits* SIMON *again, viciously.*

MAL: Say that again. Come on, baby-face. You don't even know what it's for!

> SIMON *lunges at* MAL. *They grapple, kick and throw punches in what is a very violent and virulent fight. They fall to the floor wrestling and screaming abuse.* ROD *enters.*

ROD: Cut it out, you two!

> *He tries to separate the two of them but is kicked in the stomach by* MAL *and is winded.* MAL *and* SIMON *now turn on* ROD *and beat him up with fists and boots. He drags the two of them to the floor with him.* HELEN *enters. They continue to grapple for a while then realise that she is present, and sheepishly pick themselves up off the floor. She stands and watches as they tidy themselves up and recover. Pause.*

HELEN: I've come to say goodbye.
MAL, SIMON & ROD: [*together*] What?!
HELEN: I'm leaving.
SIMON: But you've only been here a few days.
HELEN: I know.
MAL: But you haven't given us time to get to know you.
HELEN: I thought you'd understand.
MAL, SIMON & ROD: [*together*] But we don't.

> *Pause. Silence. They stare at her and try to say something but can't.*

HELEN: Goodbye.

> *She turns and walks out. Pause. They stand still. After a while they move around and tidy up in silence, picking up chairs, arranging things on the table, etc., but keeping well apart.*

MAL: [*eventually*] I know, let's go to that pub in the hills and get drunk!
ROD: Brilliant!
SIMON: Good idea.
MAL: Really write ourselves off!
ROD: We'll stay all night.
MAL: As *bona fide* travellers.
ROD: We'll demolish their entire bloody supply.
MAL: Pissed as parrots!
ROD: Paralysed!
MAL: Let's go up in the Valiant. I'll thrash it to death. Bugger driving it in!
SIMON: No. Let's go separately in our own cars. Last there has to shout all

night, or buy two dozen Aristotles.
MAL: Let's go!
ROD: Which way?
MAL: The same way we went last time, naturally.
SIMON: No shortcuts?
MAL: No shortcuts.
ROD: The same route for everybody. It's easier that way.
MAL: Let's go!

They stand still. Darkness.

THE END

DIMBOOLA

Menu

Soup

Bœuf Derrière (ox-tail)
Brodo Tomato
Mulligatawny

Main Course

Poule à la Wimmera with Sauce Mysterioso
Bœuf Arrosto Frigide
   with
Potatoes and Peas
   and
Various Salads

Dessert

Blanc Mange Jeparit
Trifle
Compote de Fruites Mixed

Dimboola was first performed by The Australian Performing Group at La Mama, Melbourne, on 6 July 1969 with the following cast:

Graeme Blundell, Meg Clancy, Peter Cummins, Brian Davies, Lindy Davies, Kerry Dwyer, Jon Hawkes, Robin Laurie, Rod Moore, Kim O'Leary, Martin Phelan, John Romeril, Margot Smith and Bruce Spence

Music by Semblance of Dignity

Directed by Graeme Blundell
Designed by Michael Hudson

Dimboola received its first professional production, by The Australian Performing Group at The Pram Factory, Melbourne, on 25 April 1973 with the following cast:

MORRIS MCADAM	Bruce Spence
MAUREEN MCADAM	Fay Mokotow
DARCY DELANEY	Wilfred Last
APRIL DELANEY	Rosslyn De Winter
ANGUS MCADAM	Tim Robertson
FLORENCE MCADAM	Jan Friedel
FATHER PATRICK O'SHEA	Charles Kemp
DARYL DUNN	Bill Garner
SHIRL	Kerry Dwyer
ASTRID MCADAM	Evelyn Krape
HORACE MCADAM	Peter Cummins
MAVIS MCADAM	Judith Kuring
AGGIE MCADAM	Eileen Chapman
LEONARDO RADISH	Robert Meldrum
MUTTON	Jack Charles
BAYONET	Max Gillies

Lionel Driftwood & His Pile-Drivers: Dick Duffy, Lorraine Milne, Chris Finch, John Rhodes, Stuart Robinson

Directed by David Williamson
Designed by Jack Hibberd and Soosie Adshead
Music by Lorraine Milne
Lighting by Geoffrey Milne
Photographs by Ian McKenzie

CHARACTERS

AT THE OFFICIAL TABLE:

MORRIS MCADAM (MORRIE), the bridegroom
MAUREEN MCADAM (REEN), the bride
DARCY DELANEY (DARKIE), father of the bride
APRIL DELANEY (JUNE), mother of the bride
ANGUS MCADAM (KNOCKA), father of the groom
FLORENCE MCADAM (FLORRIE), mother of the groom
FATHER PATRICK O'SHEA, parish priest
DARYL DUNN (DANGLES), best man
SHIRL, bridesmaid
ASTRID MCADAM, flower girl

INVITED GUESTS:

HORACE MCADAM (HORRIE), uncle of the groom and father of Astrid
MAVIS MCADAM, aunt of the groom and wife to Horace
AGGIE MCADAM, spinster cousin to the McAdams

UNINVITED GUESTS:

BAYONET, a local wit and drunk
MUTTON, a local drunk and wit

THE BAND

'Lionel Driftwood and the Pile Drivers', a group preferably composed of saxophone, piano and drums, with possible addition of violin.

LEONARDO RADISH, a reporter

Original music and lyrics for *Dimboola* can be obtained from Bryson Agency Australia Pty. Ltd., P.O. Box 226 Flinders Lane P.O., Melbourne, 8009, Victoria, Australia; phone: 613.9620.9100; fax: 613.9621.2788; email: agency@bryson.com.au. Performance rights will need to be sought in advance.

A Mechanics' Institute hall.

The guests have gathered for a wedding reception.

They are greeted at the door or foyer by the parents of the bride and groom, etc. and are served with dry sherry as they chat and peruse the table laden with gifts.

The sounds of LIONEL DRIFTWOOD *and his ensemble can be heard warming up next door. After a while the guests are ushered into the main hall and seat themselves at suitably prepared tables. The band plays on, bottles are opened. Talk and laughter. Waiters and waitresses abound. 'Here Comes the Bride' is struck up by the band. The* OFFICIAL PARTY *enters, led by the* BRIDE *and* BRIDEGROOM.

There is much chat and disorder as MAUREEN *and* MORRIE *make their way to the table.* MUTTON *and* BAYONET *sneak in from outside where they have probably annoyed guests as they arrived.*

(N.B. Any number of dances can be interpolated into the action… they should include the guests as is usual.)

MAUREEN: Where do I sit?
DANGLES: On your ring.
DARKIE: Tightest fit in the country, eh Morrie?
MAUREEN: Fun-nee.
APRIL: No fighting you two, for God's sake.
MORRIE: Nice turn-up.
FATHER O'SHEA: Behind the cake, Maureen, on the left of Morris.
MORRIE: Where do I sit?
KNOCKA: On the right of Reen.
FLORENCE: Come on, no funny buggers. Everyone settle down.
SHIRL: The guests is waitin'.
MORRIE: Nice turn-up.

> *After a while they settle into seats at the official (trestle) table. The order from left to right is* ASTRID, FATHER O'SHEA, APRIL, DARKIE, MAUREEN, MORRIE, SHIRL, DANGLES, FLORENCE *and* KNOCKA. MAVIS *sits at a small table in front of the left end of the official table.* AGGIE *is put at another small table near the right end of the official table—she is upset at not being on the official table.* MUTTON *and* BAYONET *appropriate to themselves a small table in amongst the body of guests.*

MUTTON: Never seen such a performance! Is everything under control up there, Darkie?
FLORENCE: Ignore them!
BAYONET: I'll put me money on Father Pat!
MUTTON: Has the brewery been contacted?
BAYONET: Take it away, Lionel!
MUTTON: May he have many more!
FLORENCE: Who on earth invited them?
BAYONET: I heard that!
MUTTON: We're here to see that the liquor laws are correctly enforced.
AGGIE: It's a disgrace!
BAYONET: I agree, Agatha. The guests are entitled to the draught product.
MUTTON: It's a flagrant infringement of the beverage by-laws!
BAYONET: The cold keg clause emphatically states—
KNOCKA: Shut up, you two!
BAYONET: [*to* KNOCKA] Who brought you?
MUTTON: Where's your permit?
AGGIE: It's a disgrace!
FLORENCE: Puts the whole occasion in bad odour.

MUTTON and BAYONET produce loud flatulent sounds.

BAYONET: Control yourself, Agatha.
MUTTON: Puts the whole occasion in bad odour.
FATHER O'SHEA: Come on, chaps. Quieten it down a bit.
DANGLES: Well, let's crack a few.
BAYONET: Keep them coming, Dangles.
MUTTON: I'll have to inspect each bottle.
DARKIE: There's nothing but beer. It's that or nothing.
BAYONET: What?! Wait till I report this to the authorities.
AGGIE: Do you have to shout like that?
MUTTON: Put a cork in it, Aggie.

Bottles of beer are opened at the table and glasses poured.

FATHER O'SHEA: [*elated*] I certainly needed that. Nice drop.
APRIL: You've earned it, Father.
FLORENCE: Yeah. It must be hot work under those costumes.
ASTRID: Does God dress up like that?
FLORENCE: Shhh!
SHIRL: Jeez, isn't the hall decorated beaut?
APRIL: Yeah. Mr and Mrs Bandusiae and her young Phonse worked on it all arvo. Notice the predominance of green, Father?
FATHER O'SHEA: It's a beautiful colour.

MORRIE: Nice turn-up.
FLORENCE: So is orange.
MUTTON: I'm as parched as a parrot!
AGGIE: And you squawk like one.
MUTTON: Joke, Bayonet.
BAYONET: Where? Where?
MUTTON: Aggie.
BAYONET: What's got into you, Agatha?
AGGIE: You.
BAYONET: Not likely.
MUTTON: You old shit-stick.
AGGIE: [*shrieking*] Angus!
KNOCKA: Yes, Agatha?
AGGIE: Do something about these animals!
KNOCKA: What animals?
MUTTON: Produce your permits, everybody!
BAYONET: Everybody must have a permit!
MUTTON: Government orders!
BAYONET: The Amber Fluid Act!
MUTTON: The Liquid Law!
BAYONET: All mouths must be examined!
MUTTON: And other connected organs!
BAYONET: Permits!
MUTTON: Permits!
AGGIE: Perverts!

> HORRIE *staggers in, drunk, wearing fawn FJs with the trouser-ends held in by bicycle clips. There is a brief pause and silence as he stands swaying, attempting to focus.*

BAYONET: Talking of perverts.
MUTTON: And animals.
HORRIE: Greetings and salutations!
BAYONET: One of us.
MAVIS: [*from her table at the front*] Horace! Come here and sit down!
SHIRL: Jeez, here's trouble.
MORRIE: Nice turn-up.
DANGLES: Would you like a drink to get you in the mood, Horrie?
DARKIE: Just a starter.
HORRIE: What a pack of possums you've turned out to be. Starting without me.
MAVIS: Sit down, Horace.

FATHER O'SHEA: Good evening, Horace. We missed you at the ceremony.
AGGIE: Some of us did.
HORRIE: I was there, turning pages for the organist. Honest.
SHIRL: There was no organist.
HORRIE: So what? I still turned pages for him!

He laughs enthusiastically at his own joke.

KNOCKA: Grab a pew, Horrie.
HORRIE: Thank you, Angus. Is everything under control? Why, there's Lionel. How is it, Lionel? Getting your share? Perhaps I could set things in motion with a rendition of—
MAVIS: Shut up and sit down!
HORRIE: Christ, I only hope there's some left. Some lubrication for the voice. I can see I'm going to bear the burden of tonight's entertainment. Hell, there's Mutton! [*He belches*.] Excuse me, Mavis. How are they, Mutton?
MUTTON: Never better.
HORRIE: Long time, no see.
MUTTON: Same here.
HORRIE: In form?
MUTTON: As dangerous as Danny.
AGGIE: Why don't you two grow up?
HORRIE: Jesus, *she's* not here?
BAYONET: Arsenic and old lace.
HORRIE: Bayonet! Who brought you?
BAYONET: Agatha.
AGGIE: It's a disgrace!
BAYONET: It's a disgrace!
MUTTON: Wait till I file my report.
BAYONET: Your what?
AGGIE: Angus!

An embarrassed pause. HORRIE *joins* MUTTON *and* BAYONET *at their table.*

APRIL: [*to* MAUREEN] How do you feel, love?
FLORENCE: Happy, I bet.
APRIL: You'll never be happier than this, love.
FLORENCE: It's the biggest day in a girl's life.
SHIRL: Jeez, isn't she lookin' gorgeous?!
FLORENCE: Pretty as a picture.
BAYONET: Congratulations to the bride and may she have many more.
HORRIE: Hear, hear!

FLORENCE: I wish they'd get rid of them now.
FATHER O'SHEA: Control yourself, Bayonet!
BAYONET: [*unctuously*] Sorry, Your Worship.
MUTTON: The report will be comprehensive.
> *Pause. Soup is brought in for the official table and guests (the audience). During this course* ASTRID *sings and tap-dances to 'Animal Crackers in My Soup'.*

DANGLES: How are you shaping up, Morris?
MORRIE: No worries.
DANGLES: Raring to go?
MORRIE: No worries.
DANGLES: A few more jars, and—
MAUREEN: He's not to have too much.
DANGLES: Give the poor prick a chance.
MAUREEN: He'll only make a fool of himself.
DARKIE: He's already done that.
MAUREEN: Whattya mean?
DARKIE: Getting married.
HORRIE: Hear, hear!
BAYONET: Time for a number from Horrie!
MUTTON: 'Red River Valley'!
HORRIE: [*on his feet*] In response to popular demand, I will now render that bawdy but evergreen favourite, 'The End of Me Old Cigar'.
MAVIS: You will not! Sit down!
MUTTON: 'Red River Valley'!
BAYONET: 'Old Shep'!
> MAVIS *has dragged* HORRIE *to his seat at her table.*

HORRIE: See what happens to you, Morrie. Get on top early, son.
ASTRID: Daddy's drunk.
FLORENCE: It's disgraceful! A grown man.
APRIL: Sorry, Father. Horace is not usually as bad as this.
BAYONET: A lie!
KNOCKA: Horace is sober tonight.
DARKIE: This is not normal, Father.
MAVIS: [*to* DARKIE *and* KNOCKA] Why don't youse shut up?
SHIRL: Jeez, ain't this awful?
AGGIE: He is a secret drinker, Mavis. It must be brought into the open.
FATHER O'SHEA: About as secret as Satan.
MAVIS: Don't talk to me, you bloody old crow!
AGGIE: Angus!
BAYONET: Three cheers for Morrie!

MUTTON: You little dominator, Morrie!
BAYONET: The Colonel will be very pleased.
MUTTON: Urine samples will have to be taken.
HORRIE: [*staggering to his feet*] I endorse those remarks and furthermore—
MAVIS: Shut up and sit down!
MUTTON: They must be hot.
BAYONET: An opening number from Horrie!
HORRIE: Thank you. Lionel…
MORRIE: Nice turn-up.
HORRIE: Lionel, make it 'On a Slow Boat from China'.

> *The* BAND *launches into this number and* HORRIE *sings. He is, however, soon hauled back to his seat by* MAVIS.

MAVIS: Stop making an idiot of yourself.
HORRIE: Take note of this, Morrie. Assert your authority early, son.
MUTTON: The Premier himself tasted the sample.
BAYONET: He sampled it.
DARKIE: Shut up, you two, for Christ's sake!
KNOCKA: Or you'll sample something outside.

> MUTTON *and* BAYONET *reply with crude sounds and gestures—a routine—then continue an exchange in the background. Pause.*

FLORENCE: At least they're happy, June.
APRIL: It's no funeral.
SHIRL: That's a fact. [*To* MORRIE] It's no funeral, Morrie.
MORRIE: No worries.
FATHER O'SHEA: Very gay.
FLORENCE: You have to join in. It's a special occasion. Wonder what time Dr Silverside will come?
APRIL: Wonderful of him to accept, wasn't it?
FLORENCE: Such a nice man. Very respected right through the district. A real gentleman. The only man to cure Valerie's itch.
KNOCKA: [*to* FLORENCE] Shhh!

> *An embarrassed pause.*

DARKIE: Come on, Morrie. You're dragging your bloody anchor there. Pathetic performance for a young colt.
MORRIE: No worries.
KNOCKA: Give him a chance.
MAUREEN: He's gotta make his speech yet.
DARKIE: So have I.
APRIL: Spare us from that.

SHIRL: He's just savin' himself up.
MORRIE: No worries.
DANGLES: The big event.
HORRIE: Take my advice, Morris. From a man who knows, leap into the driving seat early and dictate the play right from the word go. That's it in a nutshell, son. They drive you to the bottle otherwise, chief.
MAVIS: Why don't you shut your big trap?!
KNOCKA: He only opens it to swallow.
MUTTON: The story of our lives, eh Bayonet?
BAYONET: True, Mutton, true. Driven to it.
MUTTON: Life has passed us by.
BAYONET: Cruel.
AGGIE: As you two were not invited and are now destroying the evening, I think you should leave, immediately.
BAYONET: Drop dead, you old goanna.

Pause. MORRIE *glares at* BAYONET.

MAUREEN: [*to* MORRIE] Everybody seems to be enjoying themselves.
MORRIE: Enormous.
MAUREEN: Good turn-up.
SHIRL: Jeez, I feel real beaut. It's going straight to my head.
DARKIE: You're right tonight, Dangles.
MORRIE: No worries.
KNOCKA: He's a moral.
DARKIE: Watch Dangles tonight, Shirl.
KNOCKA: He'll be a real handful.
DARKIE: More than you could handle, Shirl.
SHIRL: Don't bet on it. He's a boy on a man's errand.
MAUREEN: [*to* DANGLES] Shirl's real experienced.
DANGLES: That's how I like them.
DARKIE: Driven in.
KNOCKA: We drive 'em in and you drive 'em out, eh Father?!
FATHER O'SHEA: That's one way of putting it, Angus. How about one of you driving a full bottle into my empty glass?
HORRIE: [*filling* O'SHEA's *glass*] As pure as the driven snow.

   MAVIS *exits*

BAYONET: When's Dr Porterhouse coming?
HORRIE: Dr Liverwurst, I presume?
MUTTON: A number from Horrie!
HORRIE: [*standing*] I thank you, Lionel—'Red River Valley'.

The BAND *breaks into the number and* HORRIE *sings with great emotion. The official table and all the guests sing.*

MUTTON: Bravo! Bravo!
BAYONET: Beautifully rendered, Horace.
MAVIS: [*entering, to* HORRIE] Just wait until I get you home!
BAYONET: Hang one on her, Horrie!
HORRIE: I wouldn't pee on her.
ASTRID: Isn't my dad funny?
FLORENCE: It's a disgrace!
AGGIE: Throw them all out! They are drunk and foul-mouthed.
BAYONET: What's wrong with that, you old cancer case?
MUTTON: What's a wedding to a wowser?
BAYONET: The opposite to a funeral.
MUTTON: Exactly.
AGGIE: Angus!
BAYONET: Angus!
MUTTON: Angus!
FLORENCE: It's a downright disgrace! Why don't you do something about them, Angus?
KNOCKA: They're not worrying me, Florrie.
FLORENCE: We're terribly sorry, Father.
FATHER O'SHEA: They're not worrying me.
ASTRID: Mummy, I want to have a wee.
MAVIS: Shhh! Don't tell the world.
MUTTON: A toast to the Queen!
BAYONET: I wish to pay my respects to the Colonel.
FLORENCE: Father O'Shea is the Master of Ceremonies. Let him run things.
MUTTON: May she have many more!
HORRIE: [*standing*] Ladies and gentlemen, allow me—
MAVIS: Sit down!
ASTRID: Mummy, I'm wetting my pants.
HORRIE: I wish to make an announcement.
SHIRL: Jeez, ain't it awful?
ASTRID: It's running down my leg.
SHIRL: I'll take her out, Mrs McAdam.
DANGLES: Running away from me, Shirl?
SHIRL: Why should I? You've got nothing I'm frightened of.
DARKIE: The word's 'round, Dangles.
KNOCKA: You're not even a starter, Dangles.
SHIRL: [*leaving with* ASTRID] I've heard.
DANGLES: Don't you believe it! Thirty wet towels. Bath towels too, no bloody hand towels.

FATHER O'SHEA: Dickies.

General laughter. Pause.

MORRIE: Nice turn-up.
KNOCKA: Jesus, never thought I'd hear a reverend say something like that. Especially a mick one.
DARKIE: Told you he was a good bloke.
AGGIE: It's a disgrace. I knew we should've had the wedding at St Basil's with the Reverend Potts officiating.
BAYONET: The Reverend Potts.
MUTTON: That old queer.
AGGIE: How dare you? One of the cloth, consecrated…
BAYONET: What?
AGGIE: Consecrated.
MUTTON: Concentrated.
BAYONET: We all know what he concentrates on.
MUTTON: Always points his great parsnip at the choirboys.
AGGIE: Angus!
HORRIE: [*elated at his own wit*] A parsimonious parsnip.
FATHER O'SHEA: Parse the bottle please.
BAYONET: [*reciting*] There once was a Reverend parson
Loved by all in the parish of Karson
However, his love for a boy in the choir
Grew to an uncontrollable fire,
And led to the abominable crime of arson.

He pinches AGGIE *on the bum.*

MUTTON: Brilliant! Silence, please. I now wish to tell a joke.
AGGIE: Father, as a disciple of Christ I demand that you squash these blasphemies.

FATHER O'SHEA *belches.*

DARKIE: Well said, Patrick.
FATHER O'SHEA: Never catch me defending a purple-pissing Protestant.
AGGIE: [*triumphantly*] See!
FATHER O'SHEA: Or a parsimonious Pom.
HORRIE: Hey, that's my word!
AGGIE: Horace and Angus, don't stand for these insults.
HORRIE: I'm Scots and proud of it.
MAVIS: Full of it.
KNOCKA: I think you've gone a bit too far, Father.

AGGIE: Hear, hear!
FLORENCE: I agree with Angus.
KNOCKA: I think an apology would be in order.
DARKIE: You're not serious, are you, Angus?
KNOCKA: 'Course I am, mate.
DARKIE: Christ, I've heard the lot. Since when did you become religious?
KNOCKA: It's the principle of it, Darcy.
DARKIE: Piss on principles! What are they?
BAYONET: Yeah. What are they?!
MUTTON: They're what drive the Reverend Potts into action every Sunday.
FLORENCE: Shut up, you bastards!
APRIL: That's lovely.
MAUREEN: Jeez, ain't it woeful?
DANGLES: Come on, calm down.
KNOCKA: Father, I'd like you to take back what you just said.
FATHER O'SHEA: *Ite missa est.*
KNOCKA: What did he say?
DARKIE: He just apologised in Latin.
MORRIE: No worries.
KNOCKA: I'd like to hear it in the Queen's English.
AGGIE: Not in that pagan tongue!
HORRIE: [*standing*] Now I'd like to render—
DARKIE: [*to* KNOCKA] You'll get your face pushed in.
KNOCKA: Come outside and say that.
DANGLES: Break it up, you two.
FLORENCE: Job him one, Angus.
KNOCKA: Come outside, you bludger!
DARKIE: Say that again.
KNOCKA: Bludger!
DARKIE: You asked for it.

They scuffle.

APRIL: [*to* FLORENCE] Why don't you shut up, and stop egging them on?
FLORENCE: Whose bloody fault is it?!
APRIL: That old bitch, Aggie.
FLORENCE: Don't be a moron.
APRIL: Job him, Darcy.
FLORENCE: Smash him, Angus!
DANGLES: Outside, for Christ's sake.
AGGIE: Teach that Catholic filth a lesson, Angus.

DANGLES *has separated the two, and is guiding them to the door.*
MUTTON *and* BAYONET *have moved to the front and are with* DARKIE

and KNOCKA. FATHER O'SHEA *continues to drink and ignores the fight, being fairly drunk and preoccupied.*

BAYONET: In the red corner we have—
MUTTON: [*raising* DARKIE'*s hand*] Cardinal Carrot!
BAYONET: And in the white—
MUTTON: [*raising* KNOCKA'*s hand*] Parson parsnip!
KNOCKA: Just wait till I get you outside, mug.
DARKIE: Your bark's bigger than your bite.
KNOCKA: All micks are as weak as piss!
DARKIE: We'll see about that, you bloody wowser!
KNOCKA: Wowser!
DARKIE: And a goat-riding Mason!
KNOCKA: At least I don't pee in the Pope's pocket!
DANGLES: [*pushing*] Out the door and settle it.
DARKIE: Right, you poxy Presbyterian!

They go out, not before one of them punches DANGLES *in the groin.*

DANGLES: [*shouting after them*] And don't come back until it's settled!
HORRIE: Time for a song! Lionel! Let it be 'South of the Border'.
MUTTON: No hitting below the pelt.

HORRIE *sings with the* BAND. APRIL *and* FLORENCE *still argue, with* AGGIE *joining in.* MUTTON *and* BAYONET *go into a boxing routine.* HORRIE *finishes off his song with great volume; everybody listens and applauds.*

MAUREEN: [*crying*] It's awful, what a wedding.
MORRIE: No worries.
DANGLES: [*back at the table*] Cheer up, Reen, it'll seem beaut tomorrow. Sock another one down.
MAUREEN: Horrie's in fine voice. I suppose that's something.
HORRIE: I thank you. That was only one to warm up on.
MAVIS: Sit down.
AGGIE: You're a pain in the neck, Horace.
HORRIE: Why don't you shut your beak, you old vulture?
MUTTON: [*making his way back to his seat, as is* BAYONET] Well rendered, Horrie.
BAYONET: I would like to extend a vote of thanks to the Colonel.
HORRIE: On behalf of the management, I would like to apologise for the slight break in the program, but with the timely intervention of Lionel and myself—
MAVIS: [*grabbing* HORRIE] Shut up and sit down, you fool!

They struggle. SHIRL *and* ASTRID *enter.* MAVIS *and* HORRIE *sheepishly separate.*

ASTRID: I did poo, Mummy.

MAVIS: Shhh! Do you have to broadcast it?

ASTRID: Well, I did!

MAVIS: Hold your tongue!

SHIRL: Jeez, it wasn't half a battle. Like forcing a pumpkin through a knot-hole.

ASTRID: Shirl did too. After me, she did. She made more stink than me.

DANGLES: Charming.

MAVIS: That's quite enough from you, young miss. Go back to your possie and hold your tongue.

They go back to their seats.

MUTTON: A hand for the girls!

BAYONET: The Colonel will be very pleased.

HORRIE: Silence please! Father Patrick, members of the bridal troupe, ladies and gentlemen, eminent citizens and fellow artists. I have an announcement to make.

APRIL: Father O'Shea is Master of Ceremonies, Mr McAdam.

HORRIE: I know that. If I have your permission, Your Grace?

FATHER O'SHEA *is on his way out to relieve himself.*

FATHER O'SHEA: [*vaguely*] Certainly, my son.

O'SHEA *leaves.*

HORRIE: I wish to thank you, one and all, for making this occasion both possible and worthwhile. It was well worth the effort.

FLORENCE: Is that all?

HORRIE: Of course.

FLORENCE: You're making a spectacle of yourself.

AGGIE: He always does with an audience. A show-pony.

HORRIE: I would also like to extend to everyone a very hearty and heartfelt welcome!

Loud applause and comments from MUTTON *and* BAYONET. *Pause.*

DANGLES: [*to* SHIRL] How's your knot-hole?

SHIRL: Fun-nee! Not for you, mate.

DANGLES: What's not for me?

SHIRL: I'm not telling you!

DANGLES: The most notorious notch in the neighbourhood.

SHIRL: You've got a dirty mind.

DANGLES: Correct weight. It's the only way to do the dirty deed. Unless you take out a licence like Morrie here.

MORRIE: Eh?
DANGLES: No worries now, eh Morrie?
MORRIE: No worries.
DANGLES: Morning, noon and night.
MORRIE: No worries. Morning, noon and night.
MAUREEN: What are they talkin' about, Shirl?
SHIRL: It's not nice.
DANGLES: She loves me, she loves me not.
SHIRL: It's all they can think about.
DANGLES: Knock it off, Shirl. Anybody'd think you'd never blotted your copybook. It's covered with more than ink. I've seen the green stains on your strides.
SHIRL: Why don't you shut your trap?
DANGLES: Shirl's very religious. Thinks of nothing else. We know all about you, Shirl. Who's for a burl with Shirl?
SHIRL: You rotten, dirty bastard.

She slaps his face.

[*Crying*] You asked for that.
DANGLES: You bitch.
MORRIE: No worries.
MAUREEN: Ignore him, Shirl. You should be ashamed of yourself, Dangles. It's awful. This is supposed to be a festive occasion.
HORRIE: It's as festive as a fart! Join in, folks.
FLORENCE: For God's sake, stop fighting up there.
MAUREEN: It's all over now, Mrs McAdam.
APRIL: Weird old wedding.
FLORENCE: Knew there should have been less grog.
BAYONET: I heard that!
MUTTON: [*to* FLORENCE] Where's your permit?
FLORENCE: Drop dead.
MUTTON: Everybody must have a permit!
FLORENCE: I wish the Reverend Potts was here.
AGGIE: Indeed. Then this rabble would have been put down long ago. I have never been exposed to so much smut and filth.
MUTTON: [*to* AGGIE] Where's your permit?
BAYONET: Everybody must produce their permit. Government regulations.

BAYONET *and* MUTTON *move amongst the guests demanding to see their permits, keeping up a stream of verbiage on regulations, laws, bureaucracy, etc.*

APRIL: [*standing*] Dr Silverside is late.
FLORENCE: [*standing*] Expect he's been delayed. He's a very busy man.

Very clever and generous. The only man to cure Valerie's itch. He's only a distant relative, you know.

APRIL: Can't say I've clapped eyes on him.

They move to the front of the table.

FLORENCE: He's very handsome. Pops in on a Sunday occasionally on his way to visit Valerie. She lives in the Western District, you know. Speaks five languages.

APRIL: Who, Valerie?

FLORENCE: No, Doctor Silverside.

APRIL: Gosh.

FLORENCE: Photographic memory. Got a mind like a Box Brownie. Speaks Italian, Spaniel, Cretin, Greek and Aboriginal.

APRIL: Aboriginal? Gosh. A mate for Mutton. He's got a touch of the tar in him.

FLORENCE: I don't think Dr Silverside would want to have anything to do with Mutton.

MUTTON: I heard that!

FLORENCE: Well, why don't you take the hint?

MUTTON: Put your meat-hooks up!

FLORENCE *hits* MUTTON *and leaves with* APRIL.

BAYONET: Hey, Mutton, look! I found this at Aggie's feet. [*He waves a sherry bottle.*] Caught her! You old trout, a secret drinker! I can hardly wait to tell the Reverend Potts about this.

AGGIE: Give that back to me! It's non-alcoholic.

BAYONET: I bet!

He has a swig.

HORRIE: I'm ashamed of you, Agatha.

BAYONET: It's cooking sherry, the lowest of the low.

MUTTON: She needs help, Bayonet.

BAYONET: And I'm just the man to help her.

AGGIE: [*pushing him away*] Don't you dare sit here!

BAYONET: [*sitting next to her*] Stop me, Delilah.

AGGIE: [*aghast*] A dirty drunk.

BAYONET: [*amorously*] Drunk, dirty and dangerous, Delilah.

AGGIE: If you think I'm going to sit here with—

BAYONET: [*restraining her*] I will not harm thee.

AGGIE: You reek of onions.

BAYONET: And worse. [*Producing a sherry glass*] Here, you must use this.

AGGIE: Thank you. Just one.

BAYONET: Delighted, Delilah! [*He pours.*] My little maggot.

The main course is served.

The band plays. Dances for one and all.

The last dance is 'The Bridal Waltz', for which everyone has entered except KNOCKA, DARKIE *and* FATHER O'SHEA. MORRIE *and* MAUREEN *dance 'The Bridal Waltz' alone, joined eventually by relations, and* MUTTON *and* BAYONET. *Mirror ball lighting.* KNOCKA *and* DARKIE *now enter with arms around one another, obviously friendly and drunk. Their clothes and hair show evidence of a fight.*

DANGLES: Here's trouble!

APRIL: As thick as thieves.

KNOCKA: We came out even.

DARKIE: Yeah. Seeing as how it was a weddin' between our kids, we decided to shake hands.

FLORENCE: We're very glad to hear that.

KNOCKA: Shut your gob.

FLORENCE: You've both been drinking more out there. Drunk before the speeches have started. It's a bloody disgrace.

APRIL: [*to* DARKIE] Don't just stand there looking pleased with yourself. You didn't achieve much out there.

DARKIE: Bitch on, why don't you?

KNOCKA: Yeah. Why don't you and Florrie go outside and tear each other's eyeballs out?

DARKIE Well said, Knocka.

KNOCKA: What a pair of parakeets.

DANGLES: Come on, you two, back into it.

HORRIE: [*standing*] Yes, gentlemen. Just in time for another item. Resume your seats.

> KNOCKA *and* DARKIE *roughly push* HORRIE *aside and return to the table where they sit together beside* DANGLES, *forcing* FLORENCE *to sit up the other end.*

DARKIE: Well, how have the festivities been proceeding in our absence?

MORRIE: No worries.

KNOCKA: Tonight's the night, son. If you have any worries, let us know.

FLORENCE: You? What a joke!

DARKIE: Listen, Morrie, old son, all you gotta do is dob it straight in.

MORRIE: Eh?

APRIL: Behave yourself, Darcy, in front of all these young, innocent people.

DARKIE: No beating about the bush, eh Knocka?

KNOCKA: Leave the preliminaries to the greenhorns.
DARKIE: In like Flynn.
KNOCKA: Up with the Jolly Roger.
SHIRL: Don't listen to them, Reen. It's just big talk from drunks.

> FATHER O'SHEA *enters, more drunk.*

FLORENCE: Father, isn't it time for the speeches to begin?
FATHER O'SHEA: Eh?
FLORENCE: The speeches.
FATHER O'SHEA: Yes. They were excellent.
FLORENCE: Christ.
HORRIE: [*standing unsteadily*] Ladies and gentlemen, may I have your attention for one moment please?!
MAVIS: Sit down this instant!
HORRIE: Drop off. Where was I?
MUTTON: Where's Doctor Silverside?
BAYONET: Three cheers for the Colonel!
HORRIE: I would like to preface my remarks on this most auspicious occasion with a round of applause—
KNOCKA: [*to* HORRIE] Shut up, or get thrown out.
HORRIE: You wouldn't turf me out. Your own brother?
KNOCKA: Wouldn't I?
ASTRID: Mummy, Father O'Shea is looking up my dress.
MAVIS: Whaaat?!
FATHER O'SHEA: Just looking for my rosary beads, Mrs Mavis.
AGGIE: Pervert.
BAYONET: They're all the same.
MAVIS: Come down here, Astrid.
ASTRID: No.
MAVIS: Come down here this instant.
FLORENCE: Go to your mother, Astrid, it's much nicer down there.
MAVIS: I'll tan your backside for you!

> MAVIS *comes across to fetch* ASTRID *but she runs off.* MAVIS *chases her around the table.*

Jesus, I'll tan your backside, young miss!
SHIRL: Awful, ain't it?
MAUREEN: Whatta weddin'.

> MAVIS *is now chasing* ASTRID *through the guests, under tables, etc.* MUTTON *is helping.* MAVIS *catches* ASTRID *and beats her on the bum. Much sympathy for* ASTRID. MAVIS *glares at everyone. Pause.*

Evelyn Krape as Astrid and Bruce Spence as Morrie in the 1973 Australian Performing Group production in Melbourne.

Clockwise from bottom left: Fay Mokotow as Maureen, Evelyn Krape as Astrid, Bill Garner as Dangles, Kerry Dwyer as Shirl and Bruce Spence as Morrie in the 1973 Australian Performing Group production.

BAYONET: Three cheers for Father Pat!
HORRIE: A song from Father Pat!
DARKIE: Come on, Father, what'll it be?
AGGIE: This is an outrage!
HORRIE: [*to* AGGIE] Shut your sewer. Right, Father, if you'll allow me to make the announcement…
FATHER O'SHEA: I will sing a lovely song that my father used to sing me. 'In Ireland, Old Ireland'.
AGGIE: I knew it.
HORRIE: Take it away, Lionel. Lionel Driftwood and the Pile-Drivers, folks.
FATHER O'SHEA: [*singing, with the band*]
  In Ireland,
  Old Ireland,
  The turf is tough on the teeth,
  As are the turnips and the heath.
  The beetroot is beyond all belief,
  The rhubarb brings no relief.
  But, by Jesus, the girls there are soft and sweet,
  And know what their young lads like to eat.
  In Ireland,
  Old Ireland,
  The winds of winter are bleak,
  In valley or on mountain peak.
  The bogs are oceans wide, centuries deep.
  No place for lovers to sleep.
  But, by Jesus, there the girls are warm and dry,
  And know where their young lads like to lie.
    Loud general applause.
HORRIE: Wonderfully rendered, Father, and most in accordance with the, er, the auspiciousness of the occasion.
KNOCKA: The what?
DARKIE: He's bunging a bit on the side.
DANGLES: Sit down, you poove.
DARKIE: Or we'll snot you one.
KNOCKA: Right between the sockets.
MAVIS: [*now back at her seat with* ASTRID] Lay off him, you bastards!
    HORRIE *sits down, crestfallen. Pause.*
ASTRID: Mummy, why isn't the Reverend Potts here?
MAVIS: Shhh! He was too busy.
ASTRID: He's nice. Always showing me his pet lizard.
MUTTON: Not to mention his carpet snake.

BAYONET: And his puff adder.
MUTTON: The old frill-necked lizard.
BAYONET: The red reptile.
AGGIE: Just as well she's young.
BAYONET: That's what the Reverend Potts said.
AGGIE: Father O'Shea is no model of virtue.
BAYONET: There are no snakes in Ireland.
AGGIE: Only idolatry.
FLORENCE: And adultery.
APRIL: What nonsense!
AGGIE: What happens to all those babies that the priests have!
FLORENCE: And the nuns!
MUTTON: The Feast of the Immaculate Consumption!
AGGIE: Where do all those children come from in the orphanages?
DARKIE: Certainly not from a dried-up stump like you.
AGGIE: Angus!
MUTTON: Our Lady of the Seven Veils!
DARKIE: Shut your filthy mouth, Mutton!
BAYONET: St Basil the Beautiful.
DARKIE: You too! Or I'll smash your boiled-bum face in.
APRIL: Good on you, Darcy.
FLORENCE: Don't stand for it, Angus.
DARKIE: [*slowly*] Will you shut up, Florence?
KNOCKA: There are two sides to all this—
DARKIE: The subject is finished. The first bastard that brings it up will get shit beaten out of him. I mean it.

    Pause.

DANGLES: It's hardly been discussed.
DARKIE: [*threateningly*] Do you want me to—?
DANGLES: All right. Calm down.

    Pause.

MORRIE: No worries.

    Pause.

MUTTON: Well, nice night for it.
BAYONET: The Colonel will be tickled pink.
MUTTON: Never had it so good.
BAYONET: Never.
MUTTON: All the regulations fulfilled too.
BAYONET: To the letter.

MUTTON: The report will be comprehensive.
BAYONET: And favourable.
MUTTON: The Government will be dumbstruck.
BAYONET: Speechless.

Pause. Silence. HORRIE *laughs nervously. Pause. Silence.*

HORRIE: [*standing*] Well, a lull seems to have descended on the proceedings. You are doubtless all acquainted with Lionel Driftwood and his able followers, the Pile-Drivers. They are the most sought-after combination in the district, and we are indeed honoured to be graced with their presence tonight, ladies and gentlemen.
DANGLES: They're being paid.
HORRIE: As you may know, Lionel has a long list of personal successes to his credit, not the least of these being his years with the Ballarat Symphony Orchestra as chief tympanist.
DARKIE: Turn it up.
HORRIE: That was before he developed his virtuosity on his current instrument which, ladies and gentlemen, we are witnessing tonight.
DARKIE: Father, how about you taking over from headless Horrie here?
HORRIE: I think a round of applause would be in order.
FATHER O'SHEA: Make it a pot, Arthur!
BAYONET: How about some more liquid refreshment?!
MUTTON: The lager that lasts!
BAYONET: The fluid that feeds!
HORRIE: I would also like to extend the hand of friendship to our Shire Engineer for his ready co-operation, no mean singer himself by the way—

HORRIE *is grabbed by* DARKIE, KNOCKA *and* DANGLES *and carried to the door.*

Hey, what?! Hands off, gentlemen!
MAVIS: [*coming to his aid*] Lay off, you bastards!

They all struggle at the door then disappear outside, from where loud shouts and shrieks are heard.

MUTTON: [*now standing at the front*] Ladies and gentlemen, I would now like to—
AGGIE: Sit down.
BAYONET: [*joining* MUTTON] No. He's brilliant!
MUTTON: Thank you, Bayonet. Quite brilliant. Yes, ladies and gentlemen, I was married once.

The BAND *plays introductory music behind the dialogue until the final stanza of the song.*

BAYONET: Five times, actually.
MUTTON: I speak of the first.
BAYONET: The worst.
MUTTON: She was the daughter of a Trentham turnip farmer.
BAYONET: How long did it last?
MUTTON: Two long weeks.
BAYONET: Two too long.
MUTTON: That's what she said.
BAYONET: You broke it off?
MUTTON: We bored one another to death.
BAYONET: You filed a separation?
MUTTON: Spent a very pleasant winter in Gunbower.
BAYONET: Your advice? Maestro Mutton?
MUTTON: Newly weds, elderly weds, twenty-year weds, all idiot conjugal quadrupeds, my advice is…
BAYONET: Never get married!
MUTTON: After that?
BAYONET: Piss off!
MUTTON & BAYONET: [*both singing*]
 A marriage is made to be broken,
 The ring you wear is a horseshoe token,
 The bonds you forge at the altar
 Are really a yoke and a halter.
 BAYONET, *as a wife, is hard at it in the kitchen, scrubbing.*
MUTTON: [*huge and domineering*] Wife, do you love me?
BAYONET: Ooh, yes.
MUTTON: Who do you love more?
BAYONET: [*romantically*] Knobby O'Toole.
MUTTON: [*outraged*] The front-end loader?
BAYONET: None other.
MUTTON: [*kicking her out*] Get out!
 MUTTON, *as a husband, is hard at it at work.*
BAYONET: [*huge and domineering*] Husband, do you love me?
MUTTON: Ooh, yes.
BAYONET: Who do you love more?
MUTTON: [*romantically*] Mrs Cockshut.
BAYONET: [*outraged*] The meat presser?
MUTTON: None other.
BAYONET: [*kicking him out*] Get out!
MUTTON & BAYONET: [*both singing*]
 A marriage is made to be tested,

The bed you share is a nest congested,
   The vows you swore at the service
   Are actually the lies of a pervert.
BAYONET: I was married once.
MUTTON: Seven times, actually.
BAYONET: All at once.
MUTTON: Bigamist?
BAYONET: Na. They was all quite short.
MUTTON: Fit in a dicky seat?
BAYONET: The lot of them. No worries.
MUTTON: What happened?
BAYONET: They all committed adultery.
MUTTON: [*aghast*] No.
BAYONET: It broke my heart.
MUTTON: Is that why you're so bitter, Bayonet?
BAYONET: It is, dear Mutton.
MUTTON & BAYONET: [*both singing*]
   A marriage is made from confetti,
   The cake you eat is old spermacetti,
   The tears you shed in elation
   Will soon be the tears of frustration.

> *As this ends,* DARKIE, KNOCKA *and* DANGLES *enter and drive* MUTTON *and* BAYONET *back to their seats.*

SHIRL: [*with everyone settling back into their seats*] Jeez, ain' it awful?
MAUREEN: Never thought it'd turn out like this.
SHIRL: Got your speech prepared, Morrie?
MORRIE: No worries.
SHIRL: It's always a help if you've got the gift of the gab, isn't it, Reen?
MAUREEN: Yeah. There's no stoppin' Morrie once he gets warmed up.
DANGLES: Bit of an athlete, is he, Reen?
SHIRL: You shut up.

> DANGLES *belches loudly,* HORRIE *and* MAVIS *enter,* HORRIE *looking very much the worse for wear.*

MUTTON: Isn't marriage a beautiful thing?
BAYONET: It is indeed, Mutton. Not to be mocked.
MUTTON: Holy matrimony.
BAYONET: Through sickness and in health.
MUTTON: Through thick and thin.
BAYONET: Until death separates us.
MUTTON: That everlasting union.
BAYONET: Extreme unction.

MUTTON: The good oil.
BAYONET: It's a holy and wholesome thing, Morrie.
MUTTON: The good oil, Maureen.
BAYONET: How are you feeling, Horrie?
HORRIE: Picking up, Bayonet. Just needed topping up.

> LEONARDO RADISH *enters, bow-tie, valise. Pause. Silence. He looks puzzled and uncertain.*

RADISH: Excuse me—
HORRIE: [*standing, delighted*] Dr Driftwood, I presume?
RADISH: There seems to be some mistake.
SHIRL: Jeez, who invited him?
BAYONET: Who brought you?
AGGIE: Shhh! Have some respect.
HORRIE: [*extending his hand*] Horace is my name, Doctor, I mean, Professor.
FLORENCE: It's not Doctor Silverside, you moron!
HORRIE: Oh. Well, who do we have the pleasure of—?
RADISH: Er, Mr Radish. I'm not sure that—
HORRIE: Say that again?
RADISH: Mr Radish.

Hysterical laughter from all.

DANGLES: What a poofta!
RADISH: I think there must be some mistake.
HORRIE: [*expansively*] Not at all.
DANGLES: [*aggressively*] Join in.
HORRIE: [*ushering him*] Join us, Mr Radish. Anyone and everyone is welcome here.
AGGIE: You can say that again.
BAYONET: The uninvited guest.
AGGIE: Thought you'd qualify there.
HORRIE: [*indicating a seat at his table*] Life's nothing but a salad, Mr Radish.
DARKIE: [*to* RADISH] Grab a pew, chief.
KNOCKA: [*to* BAYONET] Fetch the gentleman a glass and a bottle, loudmouth.
BAYONET: You know what you can go and do.
MUTTON: Right up to the kidney.
RADISH: I really must be off.
HORRIE: [*forcing him to sit down*] Not another word, Doc.
RADISH: You see, I'm from the staff of the *Mildura Trumpet*, and one of our councillors is addressing a meeting tonight, I was told that it

was to be here. So, you see I—
HORRIE: Forget about it. Meet my wife Mavis, and the little daughter Astrid.
MAVIS: Charmed.
RADISH: [*pained*] Delighted to meet you.
HORRIE: [*passing a glass of beer*] Move into that.
RADISH: Thank you.
HORRIE: [*raising his glass*] Cheers.
RADISH: [*pained*] Cheers.
DARKIE: Don't hold yourself back, mate.
DANGLES: Yeah. Wipe yourself off.
BAYONET: A friend of Horrie's is a friend of everybody!

    FATHER O'SHEA *belches.*

MORRIE: Better out than in.
HORRIE: [*to* RADISH] Nice drop?
RADISH: Splendid.
APRIL: The speeches will be starting soon.
FATHER O'SHEA: How's the supply holding out?
MUTTON: Good question.
BAYONET: Might have to call on you for a miracle soon, Patrick.
HORRIE: [*to* RADISH] What's your name?
RADISH: Radish.
HORRIE: No. Your first name.
RADISH: Leonardo.
HORRIE: [*extending his hand*] Glad to meet you, Leo. I'm Horace. Mavis my wife, and Astrid the daughter. Up there is Morrie and Maureen, the bride and bridegroom.
RADISH: [*pained*] How do you do?
MAUREEN: Glad to meet you.
MORRIE: No worries.
FATHER O'SHEA: [*drunkenly*] Cana was never like this.
HORRIE: What do you do for a crust?
RADISH: I'm a reporter.
HORRIE: What field?
RADISH: I usually write on cultural and social events.
HORRIE: Gossip column?
RADISH: Not exactly.
HORRIE: Serious stuff.
RADISH: Yes.
HORRIE: Interesting?

RADISH: I try to make it that way.
HORRIE: No accounting for taste, is there?
RADISH: No.
HORRIE: A thing of beauty is a joy forever.
MUTTON: I knew he was a poofta.
BAYONET: A pansy.
AGGIE: He's probably a very distinguished gentleman.
MUTTON: Like the Reverend Potts.
AGGIE: Can't you talk of anything but smut?
MUTTON: No.
AGGIE: What about you?
BAYONET: Yes. [*He walks across to* RADISH. *To* RADISH] Hey, I can put you onto a piece of news that'll make your eyeballs stand out on their stalks. Cultural and social. The very Reverend Potts, a local—
AGGIE: Shut your obscene mouth!
BAYONET: He has this choir made up of boys, and—
KNOCKA: Shut up, Bayonet, or it'll be the last thing you say.
MUTTON: Take all this down, sir, the Government will demand a full report.
DARKIE: Put a sock in it, ferret-face!
DANGLES: You'll get what Horrie got.
BAYONET: You bloody wombats!
KNOCKA: Say that again.
BAYONET: Why?
KNOCKA: By Jesus, don't push me too far!
MUTTON: Sit down, Bayonet, he's much bigger than you.
DANGLES: About time you displayed some sense, Mutton.
MUTTON: [*to* DANGLES] Drop dead, dumb-bum.
DANGLES: Say that again!
MUTTON: Drop dumb, dead-bum!
AGGIE: Stop behaving like children.
HORRIE: A truce, please, gentlemen! After all, this is a wedding reception, a joyous function, a celebration, an occasion of great joy when all differences and barriers should dissolve. I feel that something has been lacking tonight in that direction. The true spirit just isn't here. I might add that every effort I have made this evening has been directed towards that end, and that I aim to continue in these efforts, despite the physical opposition of some, and the nagging of others. An artist never gives up, isn't that so, Doctor Radish?
RADISH: [*taken by surprise*] Oh, yes.
HORRIE: The will to win?
RADISH: [*annoyed*] Of course.

HORRIE: [*extremely pleased with himself*] Thank you.

    HORRIE *sits down. Pause.*

BAYONET: Don't all speak at once.
MUTTON: Don't take any nonsense tonight, Morrie.
BAYONET: Lead with your left.
MUTTON: They don't call me the Mutton Gun for nothing.
BAYONET: And me, Bayonet.
MUTTON: Master of the pork sword.
BAYONET: And the beef cannon.
MUTTON: Cannon fodder, Morrie old son.
BAYONET: Think I'll slip out and fire a few rounds. Excuse me, madam.

    AGGIE *pointedly ignores him.*

MUTTON: Think I'll join you, Bayonet. [*Across the hall to* AGGIE] Excuse me, lady, I wish to water the wisteria with my weapon.
HORRIE: Watch the snap dragons.
FATHER O'SHEA: And the Venus flytrap!
BAYONET: Has that anything to do with the prickly pear, Your Honour?

    FATHER *belches loudly.*

DARKIE: Another singleton to Father.
MORRIE: Better out than in.
HORRIE: [*standing and staggering out*] Exactly.

    BAYONET *and* MUTTON *are now down the front near* HORRIE*'s table.*

MUTTON: Hexcuse us for a moment, Mr Radish.
BAYONET: The pen is mightier than the sword, Leonardo.
MUTTON: What did the rooster say to the radish?
BAYONET: I wish I were a hen.
MUTTON: And the mayonnaise to the salad?
BAYONET: All that glitters is not gold.
KNOCKA: Listen, you two circus drunks—
MUTTON: Her hair hung down in ringulets.
DANGLES: Rude.
BAYONET: If you'll excuse us, Leonardo.
RADISH: [*very annoyed*] I certainly will.
BAYONET: What do you mean by that?
RADISH: I think that should be obvious.
BAYONET: Smart bastard, eh?
DANGLES: Come on, calm down, Bayonet.
MUTTON: This bastard is bunging a bit on the side. Christ, I can't hang on any longer, [*leaping onto* BAYONET*'s back*] as Errol Flynn said to the

lady elephant. Must be off!

> *He dashes outside. Loud laughter from the ensemble.* RADISH *stands and waits for the laughter to subside.*

RADISH: Never in my whole life have I been subjected to such a display of vulgarity, crude language, obscene innuendo and immoral, adolescent behaviour. It is an outrage that this lewd, frankly filthy activity passes as entertainment. I have never been swamped by so many cliches and inanities, and never wish to be again. If I had not seen this with my own eyes, I would never have believed it possible. It is utterly shameful to find this going on in the presence of a little girl, and doubly shameful to witness its unhindered progress in the presence of a clergyman, whom I presume is in full possession of his faculties.

> FATHER O'SHEA *belches loudly.*

SHIRL: Jeez, who does he think he is?
BAYONET: What are you trying to prove, mate?
APRIL: Job him, Bayonet.
RADISH: [*ignoring them, inflamed*] The example that some of the older and more uncouth members of this gathering are giving to the young people here is to be severely deplored. This occasion should be both a celebration and a ceremony, there should be something holy about it—
DANGLES: For Christ's sake!
RADISH: It should be healthy and hopeful and sane. Not sick and diseased. Tonight has been a shock to me. I never thought that Australians could get so low, that humans could—
SHIRL: You haven't lived yet, mate.
FLORENCE: Yeah. Drop off that cloud, professor.
MUTTON: [*entering*] That mug still isn't here!
DARKIE: The bastard's trying to tell us how to behave.
KNOCKA: And how to speak.
DANGLES: Yeah. Who the bloody hell do you think you are, mate?
MUTTON: Where's your permit?
BAYONET: He wouldn't have one. Wouldn't know what to do with it if he did.
AGGIE: I think the gentleman should leave immediately in view of his offensive behaviour.
MORRIE: No worries.
RADISH: I am certainly not going to stand here and be mocked by a pack of subnormals.
BAYONET: You certainly aren't, mate.

SHIRL: Turf him out!
APRIL: Job him, Mutton!
DANGLES: [*walking around to* RADISH] Right out on your flat arse.
RADISH: Take your hands off me!
BAYONET: [*mockingly to* MUTTON] Take your hands off me!
DANGLES: [*ejecting* RADISH *unceremoniously out the door*] Back to Mildura, quince-head!
KNOCKA: Egghead.
DARKIE: Jesus, what a pain. A frustrated Salvo or something.
ASTRID: Didn't he look like the Reverend Potts, Mummy?
MAVIS: Shhh! Little girls should be seen and not heard.
HORRIE: [*staggering in, dishevelled*] Shit and derision, what was that?! This great bloody body came hurtling out and knocked me for six! I'm in no shape for that sort of treatment.
DANGLES: It was that turd from Mildura. On his way back.
HORRIE: What was the hurry?
MUTTON: He forgot his permit.
BAYONET: The Colonel was in hot pursuit.
HORRIE: [*sitting down*] Pity. He was very nice. One of nature's gentlemen.
BAYONET: Jesus.
MUTTON: Get a grip of yourself, Horace.

> MUTTON *and* BAYONET *make their way back to their seats*, BAYONET *returning to* AGGIE'*s table.*

BAYONET: Well, here I am again, beautiful.
AGGIE: You didn't have to come back here.
BAYONET: I had no choice.
AGGIE: What?
BAYONET: This is our night, Agatha. Just the two of us. I've never had the chance to say this before, but I think we're made for each other. Let me hold your hand.

> BAYONET *holds* AGGIE'*s hand with ardour. Pause.*
>
> *The dessert course is served.*

HORRIE: [*after a while*] Well, Lionel, I think it's time I rendered a number.
SHIRL: Jeez, there's no stopping the bugger.
HORRIE: I haven't sung so well in a long time.
DANGLES: Hate to hear you on a bad night.
LIONEL: What'll it be, Horace?
DANGLES: 'She'll be Comin' 'Round the Mountain When She Comes'.
HORRIE: 'Danny Boy' thank you, Lionel.
ASTRID: Poo! Someone let off a smell.

LIONEL *and the boys move into 'Danny Boy' and* HORRIE *sings. Guests join in.*

MUTTON: A masterly rendition, Horace. You have a great future.

FATHER O'SHEA *slowly and uncertainly gets to his feet.*

APRIL: Silence, everybody! Father Pat is about to begin.

KNOCKA: Not before time.

AGGIE: He's dead drunk! It's a disgrace.

DARKIE: You're not exactly sober, Aggie.

FLORENCE: You ought to talk!

APRIL: Shhh!

MORRIE: No worries.

FATHER O'SHEA: I thank you... the Bishop will be very pleased... [*he belches*] ... the winds of change... *ite missa est*... lead with your left... it gives me great pleasure to charge my glass... never lead an ace to a solo player... second player always plays low... the turf is tough on the teeth... Darby Munro, Jack Purtell, Springheel Jack, the Kilmore Kid, the coloured boy from Echuca, and Count Fritz von Hurdle the Hungry Hun from Hamburg... what a tossle... once more with feeling...

He topples backwards over his chair onto the floor. MUTTON *and* BAYONET *applaud and cheer.* DANGLES *and* DARKIE *walk down to* FATHER O'SHEA *and help him.*

AGGIE: I told you! Carry him out!

SHIRL: Jeez, what a wedding!

MAUREEN: [*crying loudly*] Do something, Morrie.

FLORENCE: Just look at him! Just look at him. Looks like a stunned mullet.

APRIL: It's just a temporary turn.

FLORENCE: It's alcoholic stupor!

APRIL: Don't be bloody silly.

AGGIE: It's running out his ears!

MUTTON: Where's Dr Silverfrost?

BAYONET: I think the Colonel should step into the breach!

HORRIE *signals to* LIONEL *and the boys, who softly play a tune.*

DANGLES: [*helping* O'SHEA *to his feet*] How are you feeling?

FATHER O'SHEA: Who won?

DARKIE: You have to propose the toast.

FATHER O'SHEA: Did we win, sir?

DARKIE: Of course.

He stands him up.

You're right now, Father.
DANGLES: Plain sailing now, Father.
DARKIE: Shut up!
HORRIE: That will do for the moment, Lionel.

The BAND *stops.*

DARKIE: [*to everyone*] Shut up!

Pause. Silence. DARKIE *and* DANGLES *make their way back.* FATHER O'SHEA *is now ready to begin. He belches.*

MORRIE: Better out than in.

BAYONET *and* MUTTON *belch in unison.*

FATHER O'SHEA: [*moving out to the front of the table, towards the guests*] Ladies and gentlemen, members of the Sodality, blood donors, cardsharps, jockeys, trainers and stewards, pillars of the Church and bastions of the steeple, it gives me great pleasure to welcome you all here today. The track looks to be in excellent condition... the fillies are frisky and the colts eager to be mounted... all in all everything augurs well...

APRIL *gets up and whispers in his ear.*

Yes, well, that brings me back to the original subject. Always count the cards... I have known the parents of the bride for some time now and heartily recommend her, I mean them, to you all. [*He belches.*] That's better... where was I? Oh yes, I've known young Daphne—

APRIL: Maureen.

FATHER O'SHEA: Maureen, yes... and I heartily recommend her to you, Mutton, I mean—

FLORENCE: Morrie.

FATHER O'SHEA: Horrie.

HORRIE: Eh?

MAVIS: Drop off.

FLORENCE: Morrie.

MORRIE: [*standing up, confused*] Eh?

HORRIE: Three cheers for Morrie!

MAUREEN: Not yet. Sit down.

MORRIE *does so.*

DARKIE: Come on, Father, you're doing mighty.

FATHER O'SHEA: I have also had the honour of knowing the parents of Morrie for some weeks now, and know them to be a holy and a wholesome couple and justly proud of their son who is, as we all know, a splendid specimen of manhood.

ALL: Hear, hear!
DARKIE: Knew he'd come good.
FATHER O'SHEA: [*loudly, raising his glass*] To Daphne.

> *Pause.* APRIL *whispers in his ear.*

Ladies and gentlemen. [*Pause.*] I ask you all to be upstanding and charge your glasses.

> *Everybody stands.*

To the bride and groom.

> *Murmurs, etc., and everybody drinks.*

I now call on the bridegroom, er... Boris.
FLORENCE: Morris.
FATHER O'SHEA: Morris, yes... to... step into the breach... may he have many more...

> *Standing in front of the official table, he shakes* MORRIE *by the hand.*

Fire away, son... never trump your partner's ace before the barrier is up.

> *As he topples backwards again,* O'SHEA *hauls* MORRIE *forward across the table onto the wedding cake, which is squashed flat. Embarrassment.* MAUREEN *and* SHIRL *wipe* MORRIE*'s front. Pause. Shouts of 'Speech, Morrie' fill the air.* FATHER O'SHEA *is left on the floor unconscious.* MORRIE *stands. Pause. Silence. He opens his mouth to speak. No sound emerges.*

BAYONET: Lower it to a roar, Morrie.
KNOCKA: Give him a chance.
FLORENCE: He is always slow to start.
KNOCKA: Come on, son.
MORRIE: No worries. [*Pause.*] No worries at all. [*Pause.*] Better out than in.
MUTTON: Not tonight, Lucifer.
KNOCKA: Come on, son.
MORRIE: I would... er... er... like to thank my parents, my mother and my father.
MUTTON: Why?
MORRIE: 'Cos.
BAYONET: What about the Colonel?
KNOCKA: Ignore them, son.
MORRIE: I reckon they've done real mighty.

> *Cheers. A chord from the* BAND.

Real fantastic, in fact.

Cheers.

Words cannot express my... er... er...
MAUREEN: Appreciation.
MORRIE: Words cannot express it.
DARKIE: Well said.

Pause. MORRIE *struggles heroically to speak.* FATHER O'SHEA *hauls himself up onto his knees.*

MORRIE: I would also like to extend... er... a vote of thanks to the Very Reverend Father O'Shea for his... er... iron-like grip on the proceedings... er... here... er... er... tonight... in spite of... er... [*terrible contortions on his face here*] ... er... ill health.

Cheers and a loud chord from the BAND.

FATHER O'SHEA: Trouble with the secret gases, Boris. [*He belches.*] A minor problem, my good boy.

Loud cries are now heard for DANGLES *to speak.*

MAUREEN: Hey, shut up, you bastards! He hasn't finished yet.
SHIRL: Yeah, give him a chance!

MORRIE *stands and opens and closes his mouth for some time. Silence. Pause.* O'SHEA *crawls back to his seat.* MORRIE *sits down, shy and defeated. 'Why Was He Born So Beautiful?' is sung.* DANGLES *stands and reads the telegrams.*

DANGLES: The Reverend Father Patrick O'Shea, Maureen and Morrie, parents, ladies and gentlemen. [*Pause.*] Well, never thought I'd live to see the day. Morrie and me have been the best of mates for as long as I can remember. And for as long as I can remember, Reen here has had her hooks into him.

Laughter. MAUREEN *is not amused.*

Her meat-hooks.
MUTTON: Mutton-hooks.
DANGLES: The lot. Morrie, wily tactician and smooth talker that he is, never had a chance. Even he couldn't hold out. The going was too tough. It's a depressing spectacle to see your best cobber reduced to this...

He gestures at MORRIE.

MAUREEN: Think yer smart, don't yer?
DANGLES: Hen fodder. A door mat. I can vividly remember the days when Morrie, mounted on his new Norton, would scowl and spurn the company of girls. Any amount of them.
SHIRL: What a laugh.

DANGLES: Well, those days are at an end. We have here tonight a new and different Morrie, and far be it for me to suggest that it is not for the better, or for the worse, if you see what I mean. I must, however, do my duty, and congratulate Reen on her success and this the happiest day of her life.

MAUREEN: [*bitterly*] Thanks.

MORRIE: Shhh.

SHIRL: What a turd.

DANGLES: Furthermore, I extend to Morrie my heartfelt and sincerest sympathies on his bereavement from life.

APRIL: Sit down, you yahoo.

DARKIE: Shut up. This is most eloquent.

DANGLES: I'd just ask, beg rather, that good old Reen there occasionally let Morrie off the hook, so the two of us can get together and let our hair down over a few jars. Finally, last but not least that is, I must compliment Shirl on looking her usual beautiful best. I only hope she's as good as she looks. Thank you.

MUTTON: Give her one for me, Dangles!

BAYONET: Full points for tonight, Dangles!

MUTTON: Let's hear it for Dangles!

Loud applause, mainly from the males. Calls for DARKIE *to speak.*

BAYONET: No more speeches.

MUTTON: Dr Gallbladder is due to arrive!

HORRIE: [*standing*] Ladies and gentlemen.

KNOCKA: Shut your guts!

MAVIS: Lay off, you bastard!

APRIL: Come on, give him a chance!

DARKIE: Ladies and gentlemen! [*Pause.*] I'd just like to say how happy me and me wife are this evening. We both feel particularly proud of Maureen and equally proud of the choice she has made of a partner, the man to accompany her on life's journey. It will not be easy. I personally feel that Morrie has got what it takes for marriage, and I assure you, Morrie old son, it takes a lot. I wish you every success in the undertaking. The spirit is willing but the flesh is weak. April and myself have become very fond of Morrie over the years and almost regard him as a son. So that while having lost a daughter, we feel that we have gained a son.

Loud cheers from MUTTON *and* BAYONET.

For April and myself this is a most conspicuous occasion.

HORRIE: Hear, hear.

DARKIE: It will not be easy.
ALL: Hear, hear!
DARKIE: It takes two to make it work.
ALL: Hear, hear!
DARKIE: It has to be a team effort.
HORRIE, BAYONET & MUTTON: [*all scream*] Hear, hear!
DARKIE: Finally, I'd like to thank Father O'Shea for the way he has handled things. Well done, Father.

Loud cheers. FATHER O'SHEA *is asleep.*

Thank you.

He sits down. More cheering.

MUTTON: No more speeches.
HORRIE: [*standing*] It is imperative that the father of the bridegroom be allowed to speak, if he should so wish, Angus?
MUTTON: No more speeches.
BAYONET: The Colonel is most displeased.
KNOCKA: [*standing*] I'd just like to say that my wife Florence and me are very pleased with the way everything has gone this evening, with the manner in which everything has been handled.

KNOCKA *sits down, abruptly.*

HORRIE: [*outraged*] Is that all?
KNOCKA: Yeah. So what?
HORRIE: Allow me then to tie a few ends together. I think that the ladies responsible for the preparations deserve some thanks.
AGGIE: You're a pain in the neck, Horace.
HORRIE: I also think that Lionel Driftwood and the Pile-Drivers deserve our warmest thanks.

Loud cheers.

They have proved to be most able and sensitive accompanists. Finally, I would like to thank little Astrid for being so pretty and sweet as the flower girl!
KNOCKA: Sit down, you drongo.
AGGIE: [*mildly drunk*] Astrid is a spoilt and stupid little brat. It should have been said years ago.
MAVIS: Hey! You bloody old crow, don't you talk.
ASTRID: [*sing-song*] Aggie, Aggie, face like a bum, dirty and daggie!
KNOCKA: Cut it out, will you? You, Aggie. And you, Mavis. If you don't keep them under control, Horrie, I'll bloody well thump you.
HORRIE: Christ, that's a bit rough.

Pause.

FLORENCE: Well, I think it's time to move.
APRIL: Yes, Reen. Get ready, love.
MAUREEN: Yes, we must go. Morrie's got a long drive ahead of him tonight. He'll have to sober up, too.
DANGLES: I told you.
MORRIE: No worries.

The members of the official table prepare to leave. There is general chatter; the BAND *plays softly in the background. The* BAND *breaks into Mendelssohn's 'Wedding March' and the* BRIDAL PARTY *leave.* MUTTON *manages to remove and hide* MAUREEN'S *wedding veil.* BAYONET, MUTTON, AGGIE *and* FATHER O'SHEA *(still asleep) remain behind.*

BAYONET: What's the damage, chief?
MUTTON: What do you mean?
BAYONET: How's it holding out?
MUTTON: [*walking to the table*] I'll investigate.

MUTTON carefully examines and drains bottles. The BAND *plays softly in the background.*

BAYONET: [*to* AGGIE] Do you feel romantic?
AGGIE: No.
BAYONET: Give us a kiss?
AGGIE: No.
BAYONET: Come on, Agatha. You know how I feel about you.
AGGIE: Leave me alone.
BAYONET: Not likely.
AGGIE: Keep away.
BAYONET: Got you, you lovely, cuddly little thing.

BAYONET and AGGIE are now in front of the official table. He tries to kiss her. She at first resists, then succumbs, her hat falling off and her hair falling down in long tresses. They fall to the floor and embrace.

Meanwhile MUTTON *has collected a few bottles in his Gladstone bag from the table. He now removes the biretta from* FATHER O'SHEA'S *slumped and slumbrous head. He dons it, collects the wedding veil and climbs onto the official table from behind and above* AGGIE *and* BAYONET.

AGGIE, *underneath, notices* MUTTON. *She and* BAYONET *get up and stand before* MUTTON, *who hands the veil to* BAYONET, *who in turn places it on* AGGIE'S *head.* MUTTON *marries* AGGIE *and* BAYONET, *opening two cans of beer and using the metal zips as wedding rings.*

He places a ring on the appropriate finger of each and blesses them. They kiss. MUTTON *gets down behind.* BAYONET *indicates to* AGGIE *that they get under the official table for a quick one.* BAYONET *lifts the tablecloth and* AGGIE *climbs under.* BAYONET *is about to join her when* MUTTON *comes around and whistles to* BAYONET, *offering him a can of beer.* BAYONET *accepts, drinks, and is led out by* MUTTON. BAYONET *looks back to where* AGGIE *is hidden, but is induced off by* MUTTON.

Pause. AGGIE'S *head appears from the other, back, side of the table. She looks around for* BAYONET, *stands, looks around again, then she sees* FATHER O'SHEA. *The violin and piano softly play 'The Sheik of Araby'. She walks across to* FATHER O'SHEA, *pauses, then taps him on the shoulder.* O'SHEA *wakes up, amazingly sober, she whispers in his ear. He smiles with a hint of lechery, picks up his biretta which* MUTTON *has returned, stands and dons the biretta, offering his arm to* AGGIE. *'The Sheik of Araby' is raised in volume and instrumentation as they leave.* HORRIE *enters and announces the final dance.*

THE END

From Ararat Gallery Dimboola *program. Reproduced courtesy Michael Leunig.*

From left: Robin Laurie as Maureen, Bruce Spence as Morrie and Rod Moore as Dangles in the 1969 Australian Performing Group production.

From left: Maureen Adamson as April, Michael Wilkie as Morrie, Mary Vincent as Maureen, Alastair Barnes as Dangles and Coralie Wood as Shirl in the 1976 production at The Hibiscus, Canberra. (Photo courtesy of Coralie Wood & Partners)

A STRETCH OF THE IMAGINATION

AUTHOR'S PREFACE

Since I wrote the introduction to the first edition of *A Stretch of the Imagination* in 1973 there have been a great many productions and most of my original remarks and admonitions now seem superfluous. Some of these productions have adopted fresh interpretative stances, diligently thought through and organic in their internal architecture, avoiding all the mannerist pitfalls. Their Monk O'Neills have ranged from a droll and rueful clown to a bilious ogre almost tragic in his ultimate self-destructiveness, providing illuminations and twists that have astonished even the author.

The dramaturgical origins of *A Stretch of the Imagination* reach back to a short piece of poetic drama, *Just Before the Honeymoon*, which I wrote as part of a season entitled *Brain Rot* in 1968. In this the two characters, Conch and Coco, obsessively re-enact a marriage-proposal ritual to animate a now lifeless relationship, to regain and relish what they have lost—if they ever had anything in the first place. The play ends with the two characters glumly enmeshed in an implacably secular world devoid of romance, dreams and spiritual adventure.

Over-sensitive, perhaps, to charges of plagiarism, I passed some derogatory comments on the ineffable Beckett in my first introduction, which I now recant. Nevertheless, at the time of writing this play, I was never conscious of Beckett, his concerns and techniques. Indeed I had not read the fellow for some years, finding his work a great silencer of creativity. It is impossible then for me to allow that *A Stretch of the Imagination* is either derivative or adaptive; it possibly explores a different mount in similar territory.

Between 1968 and the composition of *A Stretch of the Imagination*, I gathered an increasing awareness of the immense plasticity of the actor and the potentially protean nature of performance. Once the grizzled personage of Monk O'Neill had visited my imagination and the simple day-plan unfolded before me, it was this twin awareness as much as anything else that determined the text. The play thrives on theatricality; Monk O'Neill theatricalises his existence.

My own productions were chiefly naturalistic and lyric in their orientation with episodes of anti-illusionist transformation. Since then there have been at least two productions more brazen in their theatrical expressiveness, completely eschewing the reassuring idiocies of representational stage psychology. It is, I believe, in the direction of expansive yet cogent histrionics that the future of the play lies.

Jack Hibberd
Melbourne, 1998

A Stretch of the Imagination was first performed by the Australian Performing Group at the Pram Factory, Melbourne, on 8 March 1972 with the following cast:

    MONK O'NEILL   Peter Cummins

Directed and designed by Jack Hibberd
Songs by Martin Friedel
Lighting by Geoffrey Milne

CHARACTER
MONK O'NEILL

Dawn.

The present.

A small hut, dilapidated, built from old corrugated iron, with an open doorway. A four-gallon drum stands to one side of the hut. A cast-iron garden table stands some distance before the hut and supports a black sun umbrella, folded in its centre. A chair, with 'Monk' daubed in green paint across the back, stands by the table. An old alarm clock sits apart on the ground and ticks. Sunlight catches the clock. Silence, except for the clock. A bracket of snores issue from the hut. Silence, except for the clock. The alarm rings. The alarm continues to ring until exhausted. Silence. Imprecations issue from the hut, followed by creaks, a cough, and groans.

Eventually, an old man appears in the doorway on all fours: MONK O'NEILL. *He squints at the day, cheerless and sleepful. He wears a stained and tattered navy blue singlet and baggy khaki shorts. Bare feet. He crawls slowly towards the alarm clock, stiff and in pain. He arrives at the clock and slams his fist on it as if to stop the alarm. Pause. He speaks:*

MONK: Thank Christ for that.

He picks up the clock and peers closely at the dial. Pause.

Dawn. [*Pause.*] The inauguration of another beautiful day.

MONK sighs, then sits on the ground, moving his legs with great difficulty into a half-comfortable position.

My fucking legs. Corroded or something. No gristle. [*He thinks.*] It's all migrated to the skull. [*He taps his head.*] I've ossified. [*He scratches to relieve an itch, then feels his hair.*] I used to boast a healthy head of hair. No hat could contain it. [*He pats his head.*] Cancer of the scalp. I'll wake up one morning to find it all there beside me. My scalp.

Pause.

Yes. Numerous barbers commented favourably on my coiffure in the past. One, Hector De Pilo, a shearer by trade, took a snap of it… had it framed and placed it on display in his window among the hair tonics and Brilliantine. Greys is great. A good chap, Hector. Interred during the war on account of his salami extraction. Never saw him again. [*Pause.*] A lot of them around Shepparton then. Traditional. They came out with Garibaldi. [MONK *scratches the soles of his feet. Pause.*] Or was it Peter Lalor? Losing my grip on history. I once had more than a passing acquaintance with all posterior to my past.

Pause.

Not to mention philosophy. Yes. I could be quite abstract.

MONK *ruminates. Blissful. He is suddenly seized by an attack of pain in the groin. He doubles up.*

Shit. [*He stands, still bent over, and winces.*] Nature shrieks.

MONK *hobbles with awkward haste to the four-gallon drum, undoes his fly, and pees into it. The drum already contains some urine. He obtains relief. Pause.*

The organ of pleasure.

He laughs sardonically. Pause.

A doctor measured me once. Two pints. Gippsland's finest cream, he said.

He does up his fly. He peers down into the drum for a moment, then straightens up. Pause.

Nitrogenous waste. [*Pause.*] Good for the legumes.

He walks across to the table, creakily climbs the chair, and raises the sun umbrella which is weathered and bizarrely tattered. He descends. Pause.

Doctor's orders.

MONK *walks to the hut and enters. Silence. Sounds of him gargling issue from the hut. Pause.*

[*Adenoidally*] Adenoids.

Pause. He appears at the door, wearing thick-lensed glasses, and squints.

Cataracts. [*He thinks deeply. Illuminated*] Ah.

He dashes to a familiar spot, removes his singlet and drops it, then commences to breathe deeply in the manner of exercises. He stops suddenly, looking down at the singlet.

Sorry, ants.

He resumes his exercises with much flailing of arms, knee bends, and shadow boxing. He stops suddenly.

Two laps of the oval.

He runs around the table twice, stiffening and grinding to an astonished and painful halt at the end of the second circuit.

Jesus. They've locked. The compo's set.

He tries in vain to walk.

They've solidified. [*Pause.*] Doomed never to pad the earth's crust again. A fixture. I'll rot and weather just like this. A victim of the elements. A premature case of rigor mortis. [*He spits, desultorily.*] What a way to expire. Defunct. The legs that enabled me to breast the tape at Ultima, now rendered paraplegic. I could weep.

Pause.

A man should hurdle and pole vault to his coffin.

Pause. He looks at his toes, wriggles them.

Some twitches in the plates of meat. A last rally before death. [*Pause. He moves his feet at the ankles.*] Ascending looseness. [*He moves his legs.*] Agile again.

He lowers himself, with confidence, to a squatting position. He winces, immobile.

False alarm.

MONK *gingerly gets onto all fours, and crawls to his singlet, picks it up, then notices the clock and crawls to it. He picks up the clock holds it at arm's length, and reads the time.*

No.

He crawls to the table with singlet and clock. He places the latter on the table upside down. He hauls himself up to the chair, and sits. Pause.

Cruel.

MONK *feels his forehead.*

Hot.

He rubs himself vigorously across the chest and back and in the armpits with the singlet, using it like a towel after a shower.

Sweat at this hour. It'll be up to my tool by noon.

He finishes, then drapes the singlet over the edge of the shade of the umbrella and sits. Pause.

What I'd donate for an early morning squall.

Pause.

MONK *raises one leg, and farts.*

Pause. He sniffs. Pause.

I postulate a steam-producing maximum of one hundred and twelve degrees. Purgatory. Dead on three. Brrrr. [*Pause. He stands on the chair.*] In the shade. [*He peers up at a thermometer lashed to the shaft of the umbrella.*] Fair crack of the whip. Eighty-nine degrees of quicksilver already.

He sits.

Phew!

He stands.

This could warrant an excursion to Dead Dog Creek. [*Walking to the hut*] An immersion of the sizzling parts in those cool shit-thick springs.

He enters the hut. He quickly reappears wearing blue-tinted glasses, and glares at the sun.

An improvement.

Pause. He suddenly hears something, listens, creeps suspiciously forward, and peers afar. Silence. He removes the glasses.

Nothing.

Pause.

[*Salaciously*] An emu on heat.

Long pause.

Thought I might have been threatened with a visitor. [*He puts the glasses in his pocket.*] It's several years since I had a visitor. You could hardly classify him as a visitor... it was unpremeditated. He had lost his way. Stacked his Harley Davidson. Lost his way. Took a wrong turning. Don't we all? He staggered in here lacquered with dust and dung, his plimsolls in shreds, as desiccated as an old parsnip. Make yourself at home, I said. Pull up a chair. There was only one. Would you fancy a bite to eat, a beaker of something cool, a hot poultice, a kick in the crutch? Good. Relax, pal, while I repair to the Coolgardie and knock up a snack. How'd you go a Mayfair ham? You could do with a spot of salt. Bendigo pig. My lips smack in anticipation... my last tin... usually open one at Christmas... exhume a few fine memories...

MONK *enters the hut. He is heard inside, whistling and at work. He shouts from inside.*

I meant, consume. Sorry. Born and bred in the district. They cultivate a good tomato up that way. Shits on Adelaide.

He appears with a lump of ham in aspic on a plate, a screw-top lemonade bottle filled with weak black tea, and a champagne glass. He sets them down on the table.

There we are, son.

He takes a fork from a pocket of his shorts and places it beside the plate. He takes a pen-knife from the other pocket, opens it, and puts it on the other side of the plate. He pours tea into the glass.

Into it. [*Pause.*] Perhaps you'd welcome a tomato? No? A radish? Odourless onion? Broad beans? Caustic soda? [*Pause.*] All home grown. [*Pause.*] You'd prefer a stick of celery? You would. What? Yes, you heard correctly. It's not a celery district. Too hot. Too dry. Too wet. Cactus yes, celery no. The sirocco, you know. Flattens the pricks.

Pause. He stands and watches.

Difficult bastard.

Pause.

It's not often I have the privilege of a guest.

Pause.

Excuse the lack of etiquette, but what's your name? Mort? Mort Lazarus. [*To himself*] A four-by-two. I never knew there was gold around One Tree Hill. [*To Mort*] I'm Monk. Monk O'Neill. Delighted to make your acquaintance. [*Shaking hands*] Welcome to the oasis.

Pause.

What brought you to One Tree Hill? The view? Magnificent, is it not? [*Gazing afar*] A panorama of dust, ant hills, and dead grass. Naught else. Except for the occasional bull turd.

Pause.

How is it? Great. Mind if I join you?

MONK *takes the lump of meat and chews into it.*

[*After a while*] Finished?

He pockets the fork and pen-knife, takes the plate, and goes into the hut, still eating. Pause. A clatter is heard as he trips over inside, and swears. Pause. He appears in the doorway, wearing an old tennis shade. He picks his teeth with the corkscrew on his pen-knife.

It's just on dusk, Mort. Little point in setting off now, replenished as you are. Stay the night. Join me in a round of canasta, euchre, Russian roulette, you prick. Sorry. I didn't mean than. Listen, stretch out under the stars. Sleep is what you need, son. I'll fetch you a blanket. You'll be as warm as a woman. I did just that... brought out a thick old Onkaparinga... and laid it gently over his slumbrous limbs... [*Pause.*] Don't mention it, chief.

Pause.

Asleep already.

> MONK *tiptoes to the hut and enters. Pause. He puts his head out the door and whispers.*

See you in the morning, Mort. Bright and early for your departure.

> MONK *disappears. Long pause. He comes out, slowly, wearing a large hat.*

I walked out next morning and found him still asleep. Dead. A corpse. There'd been a snap frost during the night. The quicksilver was most reluctant to rise that morning. Killed off all my fucking tomatoes, too. There he was. Stiff and cold. I removed the blanket and dragged him into the sun. Thought he might thaw out, stage a recovery. He didn't. I returned, after a doomed attempt to revive the tomatoes, to find him swarming with bullants, maggots and parakeets. Quite a banquet. I tossed a few handfuls of quicklime over his remains, remembered a sad prayer or two, and lowered him into the pit of no return. Just there where the clock sits at night. No suspicious circumstances.

> *Pause.* MONK *walks across to the table, picks up the clock and reads the time.*

No.

> *He puts the hat over it. He picks up the glass of cold tea, looks at it for a moment, then tips it out. He takes the empty glass and bottle into the hut. Pause.* MONK *is heard stropping a razor inside. Pause. He comes out of the hut carrying an enamel mug, a hand mirror, a shaving brush and lather stick. He sets these down on the table, hangs the mirror on the umbrella pole, and takes a cut-throat razor from a pocket. He picks up the lather stick, dips it in the enamel mug, which contains water, looks at it for a moment.*

I used to have one five times as big as that. Everything shrinks. All natural functions fall into abeyance.

> *He feels his chin, and looks in the m.irror.*

What's the point of bristles without the ability to raise a length? Mort had a good growth that morning. Unaffected by the frost.

> *He lathers up.*

Yes. Many a female has swooned before my growth. That's not a growth, said Muriel, that's a tumour.

He chuckles, and shaves.

She knew all the correct terms… maternity matron at Leongatha Base. What a pelvis. She stretched out for me one humid afternoon… on the sands of Venus Bay. Naked. Red raw. Oozing. She didn't swoon… not Rosemary… said something about a cocktail frankfurt in a steam press… more like a cauldron was my retort. [*He chuckles.*] Notwithstanding, we ploughed up a rood or two of the beach, and she left… gave me such a nice wave from her Singer on the cliff-top. Cheerio… lovely one… I said… still supine and minus my tweeds… until the tide reached my excoriated member. Asked her to marry me. No go. Couldn't blame her, I suppose. I was a man without prospects. Then. Still…

Pause.

Muriel.

Pause.

Annette.

Pause.

Relished it from behind. Her legs were too fat.

He chuckles.

[*Morose*] They were the decades.

> MONK *completes his shave… he wipes the last of the lather off onto his hat. The rest he has wiped on his singlet, shorts and chair. He tidies up, cleans the brush, etc, and takes all the shaving gear back to the hut. Sounds of him washing his face in a basin issue from the hut. He sings 'Silver Threads Among the Gold' in a fragmented and lugubrious fashion. Pause. He giggles. Pause. He appears at the door, hair wet and freshly combed, deep in thought. He wears the glasses he first used.*

Remember, remember. Sleep. Alarm. Dawn. Pain. Locomotion. The air. The sun. Heat. [*Pause.*] Heat… hat!

He dashes across to the hat, cursing and mumbling, peeved, and slaps it on his head.

Can't afford to lose another faculty.

Pause. He claps and rubs his hands together.

To work. Only fifteen hours in which to squeeze the manifold tasks of the man on the land.

Pause.

Right.

Pause. He thinks.

Into it. Rake up the dead leaves. Apply a match. Arrr... smell the smoke... that end of autumn odour... crisp blue days... moisture in the hills... will it be this winter?... tidy up the estate... tidy, tidy... prune the willow and the yew... water the white poplar... snip, snip... Give the pelmets and sashes a lick of paint. Hose down the unit... polish, polish. Sprinkle arsenicals on the sugar-ants and aphids and weevils as they struggle past in search of a bite to eat...

Pause. He stops.

It's Sunday. According to the calendar. I presume it still to be accurate. The feast day of St Gregory Thaumaturgus, Bishop and Confessor, the patron saint of conjurers, card sharps and coffin thieves.

He enters the hut, and quickly reappears with a crude broom.

Sweep, sweep. Piss off, ants.

MONK *sweeps, erratically and arbitrarily. He develops a wheeze from the dust, returns the broom to the hut, goes to the table, still wheezing.*

Miner's lung.

MONK *sits down. He coughs and hacks for a while, coughs up some phlegm and deposits it on the floor. He leans down and examines the sputum.*

What? No blood.

He sits up, puzzled.

A sanguine turn of events.

Pause. He seizes the clock.

No. [*Pause.*] It's all too rapid. Is there no chance, clock, of a slug tempo, a *marche funèbre* for the sunset years, a last adagio into which I could pack some substance?

Pause.

Apparently not. A palpable leap of the hand. A slap on the face.

He walks grimly to the hut, clutching the clock. Pause. He walks out of the hut, pleased. Stops dead. Shocked. He wears no hat.

Merv! What are you doing here? Come to see an old mate? Uh arr. I was not born yesterday. It's revenge, Merv, is it not? Revenge. You can still harbour contempt after this time. I wasn't the only one. Oh no. I was merely the first of a string the length of a carpet snake. [*Confidentially*]

She had more love affairs than Lady Lucifer. Calm down, Mervyn! Permit me to explain the intricacies of the occasion.

    MONK *walks across to the table, takes down the singlet and puts it on. Pause.*

It was a hotter than hot evening.

    He sits down.

I was anchored in a gloomy backwater of a beer garden—the Rising Sun Hotel, Sunraysia. You said it. I was drunk… morose. My third wife had just left me. Or vice versa—bear with me, Mervyn. I was in a sad state… all psychological… the hops were having their desired effect…

    He mumbles drunkenly and drinks.

Ariadne… Miss Paddle Steamer, 1927… the best root north of Nhill… I'll remember her for her marmalade… if nothing else…

    He sings 'Shine on Harvest Moon' in a melancholic fashion.

What a fine combination… Raisin Dirt and his Dried Fruit Sextet.

    He sings and sways to 'Sweet Violets'. Silence.

Is that you, Monk? she said… Monk O'Neill lurking in the dark? Who else?

    Pause.

It's me, Dorabella. What are you doing in Sunraysia?
I could ask you the same question.
Mind if I join you?
Yes.
I said yes, Merv, remember that. I did mind.
Orrr. Cheer up. You look like you've got an anvil up your arse. Let me sit on your knee.
She did just that.
What a capacious groin.
Piss off.
I like you, Monk.
I want to be alone.
You have such virile legs.

    Pause.

Let's have a dance, Monk.

    Pause. MONK *is hauled to his feet, and dances with Dorabella.*

Hard up against me she was, Mervyn. Note that. Onc hand soft on the nape of the neck… the other cupping a buttock… licky-lick up and down my throat… tongue in the wax-black ear.

MONK *dances in silence for a while.*

Hand down the tweeds… fingers coiled around my python… tug, tug… dragged off by the skewer… behind the dunnies… forced to the turf beneath a Washington Navel. I succumbed. [*Now flat on his back*] I'll admit to that. She was most adroit… aroused my shickered member in no time… hopped on top… grind, grind… passive partner… get that down… excitations… arrrrr…! That was her… the world became a whirl of green leaves and orange cods. I spewed.

Pause. He lies on the ground.

That's when you discovered us. Stacked on a turn. Went the knuckle. Dorabella shot through, abandoning her white bloomers on a low bough. Stop it, Merv!

MONK *defends himself from punches, then boots.*

Keith Gallash in Troupe Theatre's production in Adelaide. (Photo: Penny Ramsay)

The bitch seduced me! [*Doubling up in pain*] No boots, you cunt!

He is kicked in the head and rendered unconscious. Long pause.

Unconscious for twelve hours, Mervyn. Record that too. My solicitor will be in touch. I woke up in a puddle of blood and vomit... wiped my ugly dial with the bloomers... redolent of hot cloacas... crawled to the beer garden... [*crawling*] ... and hauled my person up onto a seat.

He gets up onto the chair, sits, holding his head. Pause.

A Bayers in Bundaberg, Lance. Hey... slide a raw egg into it and a squirt of Worcestershire.

Pause.

You beat the shitter out of me, Mervyn, fractured my skull. I'm now an epileptic because of you. An excessive price to pay for a dumb fuck with a rut-crazed wife. Eh, Mervyn?

Pause. MONK *listens to Merv.*

Doubtless. [*Pause.*] I suppose so. [*Pause.*] You don't have to crawl. [*Pause. He stands.*] Shake on it, son.

They shake hands.

Well. That's cleared the atmosphere a bit. How is Dorabella these days? Eh? You don't know?

Pause. MONK *glares angrily at Merv.*

Search the house then.

He watches Merv enter the hut. Pause.

I was living in Echuca at the time. He sniffed me out. A well-appointed little bungalow in the kerosene-tin style. River frontage. Two acres of fine soil. Tomatoes. Broccoli. The odd chook... Rhode Island Reds. Yabbies. Manure. An invalid pension. What more could a man want?

Pause. Merv returns.

No luck?

Pause. MONK *listens. Merv leaves.*

Good riddance. [*Pause.*] You can't trust anyone these days.

Pause. He chuckles.

Shhh.

He tiptoes across to the hut, taps on the metal and whispers.

Dorabella, psst! [*Pause.*] She was in the tank. Up to her pelt in rain water. Out you come.

He helps Dorabella down. He admires her.

Lovely and naked too. Tickle, tickle. [*He thinks.*] I think you can follow in his footsteps. [*Pause. Nastily*] That's right. Pack your Gladstone and go.

> *Pause.* MONK *slaps Dorabella viciously across the face or vice versa. Pause. He watches her leave.*

I was ruthless with women.

> *Pause.*

Breakfast. [*Aghast*] I haven't had any breakfast. How can the locomotive of life continue to function without fuel? An army marches on its stomach. I too am a gastropod.

> *He enters the hut, pleased with himself. He appears with a plate and salt pot, puts them on the table, and leaves. Pause. He returns holding a large ripe tomato.*

A perfect specimen of the pomodore.

> *He puts it on the plate, admires it, takes out his pen-knife, sits, and lovingly quarters the tomato. He sprinkles salt on a piece and eats it with great relish.*

Pythagoras was a vegetarian.

> *He eats another piece. Pause. He stares around.*

I dine alone like Cyclops in his cave.

> *He polishes off the rest, rapidly.*

Mars is said to have stoked up on tomatoes before he slipped it into Venus.

> *He picks up the plate and licks it dry.*

The girls always loved a lick from my tongue.

> *He looks at the end of his protruded tongue.*

It used to be three times as long as that. I could part my hair with it.

> *Pause. He stares at the table, plate, etc.*

To imagine that as a young beard I dined at the most select restaurants in Melbourne. A youth of breed and starch—dapper, punctilious, well-kidneyed, etiquette itself. Knew the wines too. Must have an 1876 Château Carbonnieux with the basted salamander, anything else would be unspeakably Yan Yean, eh Jeremy? [*He laughs.*] Waiter! [*Annoyed*] Tongs, please. Pluck that slug from the endive. Thank you, Boris. Oh, could you impeach a less bumptious volume from the fiddler this evening? Now, for mains may I in all impudence suggest you plump for the hot Shlong Arabesque *à la Crème*, set off by a

Bordeaux. [*Consulting a vast wine list*] Mmmm, cellar's not what it was once. I think 1871, *ah oui*, the Château Pichon-Longueville-Lalande. Sobranie, Mimi? [*Winningly*] Oloroso, Ursula?

He takes her hand and sniffs the wrist.

Exquisite. Garçon! This table napkin is much too stiff. Another. It must adapt to the undulations of the lap, not rasp and chafe the Savile Row, you ox. For dessert, *mes amis*, it is impossible to eschew the Acheron Meringue, an ingenuous local confection in the shape of a coffin. You call that coffee, *camérière*, it's squid piss! Summon the manager. At least the saxophonist is in tune.

MONK *whistles a melody.*

Ahaa, Monsieur Épinard, I regret to inform you, but this establishment reeks. [*Standing*] Never again will I break bread or wind between these rancid walls. Good night.

Pause. He stands still.

I wonder where she is now.

Pause.

Happily married. Dead. In a convent.

Pause.

Perhaps she's returned to Rainbow, her home town, to die. I can see her now… on a wicker chair… under a pergola of everlastings… enjoying the sunsets over Lake Hindmarsh… feeding a grass parrot or two…

Pause.

Well, wherever you are, my sweet, I wish you all the best. I mean that. Dead or alive… I used to have a snap of her here somewhere.

MONK *takes out an old wallet from the back pocket of his shorts. He searches through it, produces an ancient press clipping. He reads.*

O'Neill posits the winning score. [*Pause.*] I can't remember that.

He returns it to the wallet, searches for a while, then finds a snapshot. He takes off his glasses and studies the photo at very close range.

Those eyes.

Pause. He turns over the photo and examines the other side.

[*Reading*] Pray for the repose of the soul of…

Pause. He thinks deeply. Puts on his glasses. Pause.

What a shock.

He returns the photo to the wallet, pockets it, and sits down. Pause.

He picks the plate up and takes it to the hut, mumbling and shaking his head. Silence. MONK *plays 'The Airy Bachelor' on his mouth organ. Pause. He appears in the doorway, in sunglasses, gazes up at the sun, then ahead.*

Conjunctivitis. [*Pause.*] As they say at funerals.

He walks across to the chair, climbs up, and looks at the thermometer.

Phew! [*Pause.*] I'll cremate. [*He scans the distance, in all directions.*] Alone. Thank Christ.

He gets down and sits.

One is company... two congestion.

Pause.

It was quite a relief when my last wife passed away, as they say. Not that I was there. Nor was I here. No. Yes, they gave her a fine send-off. At the city morgue. The chief pathologist, an old Xaverian like myself, was kind enough to forward me a few of her things... memento moris...

He fishes into a pocket and produces an old brown paper bag. He opens it and looks deeply into it.

A thoughtful chap... nothing too personal.

He takes out a small stone, looks at it.

Gallstone.

He puts it back, fishes in again.

Ahaa!

He produces a set of dentures, upper and lower, hinged together at the back, by fish hooks or bobby pins. He clacks the dentures open and shut.

Not a bad set of fangs for one so old... and verbose... clack, clack... often spoke in public... a suffragette someone said... agony I called it...

He tosses them back in the bag, peers and feels in the bag.

There used to be a painted toenail... gone.

He returns the bag to a pocket. Pause. He suddenly winces with pain, and doubles up.

Jes-suz.

MONK *walks, doubled over, to the drum, undoes his fly and attempts to urinate. Pause.*

[*Aghast*] I void null.

He grunts and squeezes.

Not a solitary spermatazoon. [*He does up his fly. Pause.*] What happens now? The gland has won. I could puff up with piss and detonate. Do a Henry the Eighth… swell up, curse, shout, scream, and explode… covering icons and sycophants alike in the last meal and tomorrow's excrement. [*Pause.*] How to cope.

He sits down.

Think.

Pause.

A dry hot day. Still. Not a breath of wind. Heat. Hot. The sun. An expanse of red sand. No moisture in the sky. Nor moss beneath the feet. Grey grass. Bleached-out weeds. Granules. And sticks. Fire. Fire.

Pause.

Subsist. The rest is silence.

Pause.

Grey to blue. Blue to grey. Ad nauseam. [*Pause.*] Nature's incomparable palette. [*Pause.*] Where there's life there's hope. Said the undertaker. On his death bed. [*Pause.*] He used to be a butcher. An expert with a carcase. Until he lost all his fingers, that is. [*Pause.*] Housewives always spoke elatedly of his sausage. [*Pause. Puzzled*] He never married, though.

Pause.

Ah, well. [*Pause.*] A man's best friend is his dog.

Pause.

Even woman cannot attain the high standard of companionship afforded by the dumb canine.

Pause.

A man. His dog. A man.

He removes his sunglasses.

I shot my dog.

He stands and whistles.

Hey, Cyril! She was a Queensland heeler. Here, girl. Come on.

He pats the dog.

Good girl.

He takes something from the table.

Here's a treat for you. Roast rabbit.

He tosses it on the ground, and shouts.

Sit! Sit, Cyril. Beg. On your hind legs.

Pleased, he watches the dog sit.

Good dog. Well trained. To lick and love.

He backs slowly to the table, and picks up a rifle.

Sit, Cyril. That's the girl.

He raises the rifle and fires. Pause.

One less mouth to feed.

He drags the dog off by its legs and disappears.

One less rival for my affections.

Pause. MONK *is heard whistling 'Thanks For the Memory' in the distance. He returns.*

Threw her in the creek. She was a good water dog. A natural in the liquid. [*He puts on the sunglasses.*] I wish to weep.

He enters the hut. Pause.

[*Loudly*] No!

Pause. MONK *rushes out, without sunglasses, and wearing a large farmer's hat.*

Time to till the soil, applaud growth, admonish the weeds.

MONK *gets stuck into the garden, frenetic, with pick and shovel, adze, plough, hand-fork, etc.*

Weed, weed, dig, dig. Sorry, Mort.

He continues for a while, then stops suddenly, in pain and bent over at a fixed angle at the hips.

Faaarrk. [*He tries to straighten up, bites his lip in agony as he fails.*] They've locked. [*He thumps each hip with a fist.*] It's permanent. [*Pause.*] What if I pass in my marble like this? A former athlete and tumbler. The Nullarbor springboard champion of 1919. The first to swim Lake Eyre... die stiff... at an obtuse angle... no. [*He walks, still bent, towards the hut.*] Perhaps the rigor mortis will straighten me out. Or some kind mortician.

He enters the hut. Pause. A loud crack issues from the hut. Pause. A sigh of relief from MONK. *Pause. Bottles clink.*

Sloan's Liniment.

Assorted noises.

Turps.

> MONK*'s shorts sail through the door and land before the hut. The singlet follows. Pause.*

Sorry, Mort, but they could do with some fresh air and sun.

> MONK *is heard rubbing himself.*

Arrrrr.

> *He runs on the spot. Silence. He appears in the doorway, attired in a flaccid and antique jock-strap, along with his blue-tinted spectacles. His hips glisten. Pause.*

Cured.

> *He picks up the shorts and singlet and dresses.*

The piston of life pumps once again. I look forward to yet another penultimate day. Grind, grind.

> *He walks to the table, and sits. Pause. He whistles and sings fragments of 'French Can-Can'. He gazes, with hauteur, up and down the boulevarde.*

[*To himself*] Wo ist il garçon de house? [*Studying a menu*] Garçon!

> *Pause. The waiter arrives.*

Suprêmes de Volaille aux Champignons et Truffes. Aussi, un bottle de Veuve Cliquot Brut. [*Pause.*] What? [*Pause.*] *Immédiatement,* turd-face!

> *Pause.* MONK *takes out a cigarette, places it in a long holder, lights up, and smokes. A woman of some beauty and voluptuousness appears and walks past.* MONK *whistles in admiration, and stands.*

Eh, you, madam... Je t'aime... [*Walking a few steps after her*] ... Je t'aime...! Voulez-vous une jig-a-jig?

> MONK *stands and watches her go. He returns to the table and sits down.*

Paris. 1912. Boulevarde Haussmann. South of the Parc Monceau. West of the East Cemetery. What a day. [*Pause.*] I cycled from Calais to Nôtre Dame... head wind all the way. Parked the Malvern Star up against a flying buttress and went for a swim up the Seine, introducing the Australian Crawl to the Frog. I obtained a salon on the Ile Saint Louis... met a few gormless Poles... lingered on until the finances lapsed, some seven days... then pedalled back.

> *Pause.*

I thought I saw Stravinsky one afternoon. He didn't recognise me.

> *Pause.*

I did shake hands with Proust, however. In the Montparnasse Cemetery.

Neville Teede in the W.A. National Theatre production in Perth. (Photo: Simon Cowling)

What brings you here at this time of night, sport? I said in everyday French.
I cannot sleep, he said.
Have a swig.
He refused.
What do you think of Baudelaire?
But he had gone... a shadow among shadows.

> *Pause.*

Shit! [*He takes off his glasses.*] I haven't milked the goats.

> *He dashes off to the hut, mumbling about his memory, is heard bustling around inside for some time, then appears wearing the farmer's hat and ordinary glasses, carrying a billy-can and the clock, which he plonks peevishly on the table as he dashes past and disappears. A long silence, except for the clock.* MONK *returns, puffing, with a large pumpkin. He places the pumpkin on the ground, stands and regains his wind, wipes his forehead. He sits and fans himself with his hat. He suddenly seizes the clock.*

[*Incredulous*] Midday! No. Co-operate, timepiece. You've made a mockery of my morning. Mort is very upset. [*Pause.*] Hark! Shhhh. Hear the present ocean past.

> *Pause.*

Not the tick-tock of ratchets and cogs, but a continuous and silent avalanche. We do not move forward. We merely mark time. All progress is an illusion. Our advance into a vacuum is also an illusion. So cheer up.

> *Pause.*

If time were slower there'd be more of the present to dwell upon the past. That would please me, Mort, no end... the past is something to which I always look forward...

> *Pause.* MONK *picks up the clock and puts it on Mort's grave. The pumpkin sits nearby. He returns to the table and sits. He ruminates. In due course, he sings.*

> > On One Tree Hill
> > the moon never sets
> > the sun never rises
> > because because because
> > the moon never rises
> > the sun never sets
> > on One Tree Hill.

Pause.

I hate moonbeams, dawns and sunsets.

Pause.

To imagine that I could've retired to a rich and temperate country estate. Pastures of thick and succulent grass... green all the year round. Avenues of elegant poplars. Merinos the size of stud bulls. A Cadillac. Granaries bursting at the buttocks with lucerne and newly sliced hay. A hill of bauxite. Dormer windows... the milk and honey odours at dawn of young maids... perfumes of Piccadilly aftershave, cider, and clean sheets.

Pause.

Not for me.

Pause.

They're all dead. The whole miserable pack of them. They retired to the country and died of the city. Tumours.

Pause. He stands.

Cheer up, you morbid prick. [*Pause.*] Yes. I know you've got cancer of the white blood cells, Luke.

Pause.

Max Gillies in the 1976 Australian Performing Group production in Melbourne. (Photo: Brendan Hennessy)

All right. You've got three weeks to live. Look at it from the opposite angle. You've got three weeks to die. Think of it that way and relief will be immediate.

Pause.

He didn't. Wouldn't heed the advice of his senior brother. Those last three weeks could have been extrovert and cordial, full of rhetoric and joy. [*Pause.*] Instead, the weak bastard allowed Father Asterisk, a snivelling and vulpine Jesuit, to sneak in and piously rekindle the dead tapers of guilt... with talk of Ireland and the usual slop. I intervened just in the nick of time to arrest the most fulsome death-bed recantation.

MONK *stands with a revolver in one hand, waits, opens a door quickly, and enters.*

Put down that crucifix, Asterisk.

Pause.

You heard.

Pause. He fires.

One less icon. And pocket that oil before I put one through your wrist.

Pause.

Good. Now, sisters, remove that statue. [*Pause.*] Have it your own way.

He blazes away at the statue. Pause.

I always leave the serpent intact. [*Pause.*] Get out.

He watches them leave, then pockets the revolver.

Relax, Luke, all is under control. Go back to sleep, son.

Pause. He stoops down to hear what Luke has to say.

How'd you guess? Guy Fawkes Night.

Pause. He goes to the table, picks up his hat, and holds it in his hands, about to leave.

He stuttered a few irrationalities, then slid back into sleep or unconsciousness. I left him to die alone. The only way.

He walks to the door, opens it, and leaves the room. He puts his hat on. He stands for a moment, then walks off. Pause. He returns, hatless, stands for a while. He picks up the pumpkin. Pause.

The human soul.

Pause. MONK *takes the pumpkin into the hut. He is heard inside at various tasks. He eventually comes out bearing an old Willow tray and goes to the table. He unloads it onto the table: a plate with a tomato, lettuce leaf, radishes and cold roast meat, the lemonade bottle of tea, a fork, and enamel mug. He sits, takes out his pen-knife, and quarters the tomato.*

I always eat in style.

He produces a book from under his singlet where it has been tucked in behind the top of the shorts. He props the book up, after finding his page which is marked with a painted toe-nail.

Aha! There it is.

He reads and eats, dipping meat, tomato, etc, into a pile of salt on the plate, before devouring.

Plato.

He pours out some tea, and drinks. He eats with increasing relish and pace. He chuckles at something in the book.

Good point. I concur there.

He reads on, and eats.

[*Dubiously*] Mmmm.

Pause.

Na. Couldn't accept that. [*Pause. Eating some meat*] Lovely roast emu. [*He goes back to his book.*] Wish I had this in the original Greek. Dux of Classics at Xavier 'round the turn of the century. Didn't go on with it... I was much more physical in those days than metaphysical... much more. Pity.

He finishes off his meal, drains his mug of tea. He puts the toe-nail in the book and closes it. Pause.

That's better. [*Pause. He yawns deeply and at length.*] Siesta time.

He puts things back on the tray, stuffs the book into his shorts, and transports the tray back into the hut. Noises issue from the hut. Pause. Soft music from an old record issues from the hut: Fritz Kreisler playing one of his own compositions. MONK *appears in the doorway.*

Slop.

He walks across to the clock, picks it up, winds, then replaces the clock on the ground.

Excuse me, Mort. But in my opinion every grave should boast a timepiece.

He walks over to the drum and undoes his fly.

Or a metronome.

He attempts to urinate. Pause.

Typical.

He walks across to the hut, pauses before the door. Does up his fly. Pause.

[*Gesturing*] After you, Diana.

He smiles. He sours. Pause. He enters the hut. Pause. The music becomes louder in volume. MONK *sings vociferously to the music. The record ends. Pause.* MONK *is heard snoring.*

♦ ♦ ♦ ♦ ♦

Afternoon. Overcast. Cold. Groans and execrations issue from the hut. Silence. MONK *appears in the doorway, attired in an army greatcoat. He walks forward for some distance, then suddenly stops, astonished.*

MONK: Brrrrr!

He looks at his bare feet.

They're blue.

He stoops to massage his feet.

The patio is a sheet of ice.

He crawls.

Never have I known it to be so frigid. [*Pause.*] I would not be at all surprised to see a mammoth… gallop across the horizon.

He peers closely at the ground.

No. Two ants. Snap-frozen within the ice. One's holding aloft a bread crumb. Or is it an egg? Difficult to perceive… poor little pricks. Hey, there's a couple caught in the act. Like Mum and Dad… life goes on.

He crawls forward, and reaches the clock. He has difficulty picking it up, because of the coldness of his hands. He rubs his hands together and blows into them; he wriggles and flicks them, stops, and examines them spread out, stiff.

To think that these once-supple dactyls caressed the ivories on many a Saturday night at the Saloon Bar of the Shamrock… accompanied by Cliff Treble on double bass and Les Saffo on soprano sax. No more.

Pause. MONK *manages to pick up the clock and holds it close to his face.*

[*Aghast*] It's stopped. Dead on twelve. [*Pause.*] Noon. [*Pause.*] On a day like this.

He shakes the clock, and listens. Silence. He winds the clock, and listens. Silence.

Silence.

Pause.

No time. For the moment.

Pause.

No sun.

Pause.

Perhaps it's midnight... and the North Pole has slipped south. Or vice versa... ah well.

He puts the clock in a pocket, and crawls across to the table.

Shakespeare was right.

He reaches the chair and hauls himself up. He rests.

Brrrrr.

He stamps his feet for a while, stops, and looks incredulously at them.

Forgot my boots.

He climbs up on the chair, and studies the thermometer.

Zero.

He gets down, and sits. Pause.

Antoinette.

Pause. He smiles.

How are you...? Sitting there all rugged up in a thick blue overcoat, and red woollen scarf, and a nondescript beanie down over your ears...

Pause.

Mount Buffalo. A snowstorm. A balcony. Depression years. Hand out, across the table... touch her on the glove...

He does this.

Look me in the eye.

Pause.

[*To himself*] Fuck the snow. Can't see a thing.

Pause. He leans forward.

Did you enjoy last night? [*Pause.*] No. [*Pause.*] The snow. The dinner. The dance. That log fire of sizzling pine... pancakes and cognac. Bed.

Pause.

You're not in love? What do you expect in a weekend? In a year? Ever? [*Pause. He listens. He laughs.*] Romance, yes. Love, no.

She withdraws her hand.

There is no such thing as love. It's a misnomer for infatuation, infatuation elongated and attenuated into habit.

She leaves. He watches her go. He drinks cognac from a balloon. Pause.

Dark came down. Music. Yellow windows. Fake Austrian yodels. Shrieks of agony disguised as pleasure. Or vice versa.

Pause. MONK *sings.*

> Dead cockatoos are falling from the sky
> clouds of phosphorus scud merrily by
> pterodactyls flap across the moon
> in answer to a dodo's midnight croon.

He yodels.

> Sounds of suicide echo from afar
> the oceans of the universe are liquid tar
> obese white slugs denude the earth
> two skeletons foxtrot on a field of afterbirth.

Pause. He yodels. Pause.

The only people I regret leaving behind are my enemies. I wish them well. [*Pause.*] A friend did write to me once... several years ago... sent it poste restante the Nonultra Post Office... popped in there a few years ago and picked it up... did have it somewhere on my person...

He searches in pockets, finds the clock, looks at it, bewildered, puts it face down on the table, and continues his search. He eventually produces a grubby old letter. He reads. He chuckles at something in the letter. Pause. He fumes.

Liar! [*He reads on.*] What temerity. [*He reads, bemused.*] The old bitch. [*He reads on.*] Cut it out. [*Pause.*] Yours sincerely, Ernest.

Pause.

He wants to come and visit me.

Pause. MONK *turns the letter over and studies the back closely. He discovers some writing and follows it with a finger as he, with difficulty, reads.*

Dear Mr Gulliver... I remember all the events and individuals you allude to... I am not an idiot... in particular that weekend we walked along the Acheron Way in search of fossils... yes, I recall those intemperate and... perdurable... evenings at the Recherché... a milieu thick with claret fumes and cheroot smoke, politics and sex... readings from Wittgenstein with musical improvisations by Gap Silenzio the noted bassoonist... dawns in the gutter... clutching *Ulysses*... I am now abstemious... [*chuckling*] ... please do not attempt to come the treacle with me... piss off... leave me alone... O'Neill.

Pause. MONK *returns the letter, after carefully folding it, to a pocket.*

Brrrrr! [*He rubs his hands together.*] Exercise time.

MONK *stands up and commences a set of exercises, both to warm up and maintain his physique of which he is very proud. He continues for a while, then stops suddenly as he feels faint. He walks unsteadily and weakly to the chair, sits down, breathes deeply, then stops breathing and falls to the ground. He lies motionless for some time. He starts to breathe, then stir. He sits up slowly, shaken.*

Uh... Wha?... How'd I get here?

Pause. He hauls himself up onto the chair.

Blackout... no stroke, I hope.

He moves each arm and leg experimentally.

Thought I'd croaked.

Pause.

I would like my departure from this life to be a little longer than that. Perhaps a whole afternoon. A slow crawl on the stomach to the record player... a few bright numbers from a requiem or two... a last tomato... a slice of ham... some sugar for the ants... couldn't make it to the goats... a last jerk of the gherkin... just in case... you never know... I'd like to die erect... hang up my rosary beads... memento mori, Mort... see you tomorrow today... croak.

Pause.

Brrrrr!

He climbs up, carefully, on the chair and peers closely at the thermometer. Pause.

[*Incredulous*] The mercury has disappeared from view.

He climbs down and stands, gloomy.

The end is in sight.

He walks, dejected, into the hut. Pause. MONK *appears at the door. He wears a large bucolic straw hat, pink-tinted goggles, and sandshoes. He gazes around the environs.*

[*Lugubriously*] Glad-rags.

Pause. He suddenly sees something in the distance and stiffens, then dashes on a semi-circular course.

I thought I saw something... a steam-roller speeding along, discharging red smoke.

He stops, puzzled. He takes off the goggles, looks at them, puts them on, and peers again.

Gone.

He shakes his head, and sits down. Pause.

It could've been a snow plough.

Pause.

Reminds me of the time Les Darcy and I scaled Mount Kosciusko. Les was in training at the time for his first clash with that other fine exponent of the leather, Jess Smith. There we stood on the summit, gazing across our fair land... Australia... attired only in boxing trunks and slouch hats... our bare feet commingling with the soft thin snow. Young Les, somewhat overcome by the grandeur of the khaki expanse before him, intimated to me a vision of the future. Monk, he said, one day Australia, that great nation out there of soldiers and sports and athletes, cereals and wool, will one day rule the Pacific. I believe that. England will one day lick the elastic of our boots. America will extend to us an equal hand. The Indon and Kanaka we will civilise. Out there, O'Neill, lies a germ... the germ of the future. With water and work it will breed and grow and spread into an empire of fair play and health and wealth and power, and wealth and literature.

He had tears in his eyes.

I took him by the southpaw.

Cut it out, Les. You cannot extract sunbeams from a cucumber. The lack of oxygen has sapped your intellect. Put up those dooks, and we'll go a round or two for a pound or two... it's as cold as a cunt on concrete.

MONK spars with Les, ducks and weaves with a surfeit of footwork. He curses and winces with pain as he takes a few punches... Les hits hard and low.

Above the belt, Les. Remember Fritz Holland.

The spar, now a fight, continues for a while, until MONK is floored. He lies unconscious. Pause. He lifts his head.

K.O.

MONK *resumes his unconscious state. Pause. He gets up, groggy.*

That's no way to treat a distant cousin, Les... a long lost friend... a sparring partner.

Pause.

That's no way to treat Australia, said Les, and walked off... down into Perisher Valley...

Pause. He goes across to the drum, undoes his fly, tries to urinate, without success.

This does not augur well. [*He squats.*] I'll give the relevant organ a squeeze. [*Pause. He gets up, with difficulty.*] Jees-suz.

MONK *tries again to urinate, without success. He does up his fly. He peers deeply into the drum.*

Narcissus.

He walks toward the hut, stops, and farts.

A silent one. [*He sniffs.*] I should've been a politician.

He enters the hut. Pause. A loud fart issues from the hut. Pause. MONK *plays 'Danny Boy' on the mouth organ. Silence. He dashes from the hut, without hat or glasses, across to the table, picks up the clock and studies the dial at close range, exasperated.*

How can a man organise his day bereft of time mechanical? Up at seven. Shave, shave. A scour of fangs. Ablution of the parts... *lavabo* therefore I am. Breakfast at half past. Juice of the orange... stewed prunes with my cereal... yes, doctor, I keep regular. Steak and eggs... a quick ogle at the mineral market... a first suck of the nic-stick... only one packet a day, doctor... dead on eight... a strain at stool... plop!... wish I had one as big as that... a kiss for the cook... out the door and into the GT... isn't she beautiful pat, pat, polish, polish, kiss, kiss, rev, rev. [*He sits.*] Screech of the rubber, purr of the motor down Vanadium Avenue... the music of those radials... beep, beep...

MONK, *seated, now drives an old car along a bumpy bush road.*

Only two more miles to my sweetheart's little bungalow. She awaits me. A young widow. [*He whistles exuberantly as he drives along.*] Gosh. The wildflowers are out.

He pulls up, and gets out of the car.

What a display.

He walks about, picking flowers.

Some pink fingers... and a stalk or two of erect violet... what have we here?... love creeper... comesperma volubile... that's me... [*reaching up*] ... some red box... lovely... give the fungus a tickle... some native willow for her window when I leave... you have to be cruel to be kind... ha ha... and finally a few immortelles, forget-me-nots and everlastings with which to fashion a wreath. [*Pause.*] I was romantic then.

He puts the flowers in the car, gets in, and drives off.

Not far now... arr yes, I discern a feather of smoke... drive, drive... [*thrashing along*] ... she lays a nice table... my dentures water.

He arrives, toots the horn.

Toot, toot!

He gets out, collects the flowers, and walks to the door.

You-whooo! It's Monkee-wonkeee. [*Pause.*] Caroline!... it's O'Neill... the Casanova of the peach district.

Pause. He tries the door. Locked.

Caroline!

The door opens.

Caroline. There you are.

MONK *hands her the flowers.*

Pleased to see me? Gosh, you do look beautiful. All in black still.

Pause.

Aren't you going to invite me in? The evening grows chill.

Pause.

No?

Pause.

Go away.

Pause.

She was serious. [*Pause.*] Are you serious?

Pause.

Yes.

She throws the flowers at his feet. Pause.

You're no good, she said. I want a man, not a ferret. You're about as much use to me as a pipe-cleaner.
But you said you loved me.
She laughed. Long and loud.

Pause.

Don't just stand there, piss off, she hissed.

MONK *stands.*

She slammed the door in my face. The lock shot home.

Pause. MONK *suddenly flings himself at the door, beating and kicking it.*

You two-timing fuck-witted mongrel of a slut! Open up or I'll stuff you with a fist full of broken glass! [*Pause.*] Anyway, since when have you been so choice in bed? A hole like a bowl of porridge. What you need is not a dick but a piston. Or a sponge soaked in vinegar.

MONK *picks up a flower, sniffs it, puts it in his button-hole, and walks off. Pause. He returns, and sits down.*

Pause.

The vegetables are doing remarkably well. Considering.

Pause.

When I first came to One Tree Hill there was this one tall tree. Nothing else. A hairy tree. Conspicuous, almost outlandish. Not wishing to advertise my presence, I took an axe and chopped it down. Thud. I looked at the tree... and the uproar was immense. Every cockatoo, crow, emu and rosella in the kingdom had taken to the heavens filling them with spleen and indignation. Lesser men would have regarded this as a harbinger and knelt down in supplication. Not me. I seized the old shotgun and fired salvo after salvo at the demented pricks.

Pause.

Later, I found Cromwell, my faithful old Clydesdale, nailed under the cross-bough of the tree... breathing his last. [*He kneels down.*] Cromwell, old son.

He pats the horse on the head.

Take it easy.

Pause.

A clear sweet-smelling fluid trickled from his nostrils.

MONK *feels in his pocket.*

Here, Cromwell. A last carrot.

He offers the horse a carrot.

No.

He returns it to his pocket.

Peter Cummins in the 1972 Australian Performing Group production in Melbourne.

Why didn't you gallop off? Too old. It'll take me an hour to saw through that bough. Your insides are crushed. You won't make it to port. [*Pause.*] No hard feelings?

Pause.

Dead.

He gets up, slowly and stiffly.

You're not the only one unable to raise a gallop, Cromwell. Still, I am blessed with some employment of limb. I contrive to walk. I breathe. I cerebrate. I have no soul. What more could a man desire?

Pause. He takes off a sandshoe and looks at the foot, separates some toes and peers between, scratches between the toes, takes his ordinary glasses from a pocket, puts them on, and peers again.

Aha! Athlete's foot. [*He scratches again.*] At my age.

He walks across to the drum and places the afflicted foot in the urine. He groans in agony. Pause.

Oedipus. [*Pause.*] Or was it Achilles?

He removes the foot and walks back with a limp to the chair.

A classical education is a fine thing. I'm a great reader. [*He sits.*] I always have some reading substance by my elbow at night. Yes, I brought my library with me. I enjoy a good text. [*He looks at his foot.*] Still itchy.

MONK *searches in his pockets and eventually produces a set of rosary beads, without a crucifix. He takes hold of each end of them and draws them back and forward between the afflicted toes to relieve the itch.*

[*Ecstatically*] Arrrr. That's better.

He studies the rosary beads.

Drops of blood from the Blessed Oliver Plunkett's decapitated neck. So mother said.

He puts them back in a pocket. He dries his foot with his coat.

To think that this superannuated trotter directed the winning leather in the Grand Final of 1907... or was it 1917? No matter. Now. Yes... I was in a back pocket... galloped down to the half-forward for the opposition and brought off the most elegant one-handed capture, skirted a bovine pack, bounce of the ball, dummied around the hitherto damaging Stingy Ray, bounce of the ball, shot down the flank, at which place a toey winger was rendered flat of foot by a long handball over his skull on to the half-forward line, at which place I regained the bladder, dummied thrice, bounce of the ball, weave, steadied, choice of feet, and slammed it through the teeth of goal to raise the twin white calicos and bring the crowd to their knees at the final toll of the bell.

Pause.

Fuck sport.

Pause. MONK *puts on his sandshoe. He feels in his pockets once again.*

There was something I had to remember today. I remembered yesterday.

He brings out an old empty brown paper bag with irregular scribblings all over it. He studies them.

Mmmmmm. [*Pause.*] Here we are. Of course… alter my will.

He returns the bag to a pocket and walks to the hut, eagerly. Pause. He comes out with a sheep's skull, puts it on the table and plucks a piece of folded paper from one of the skull's eye sockets. He takes a pencil, old and short, from behind his ear. He unfolds the paper, studies it, and licks the lead of the pencil. He makes a few quick alterations, finishes, looks pleased, and reads.

The last will and testament of Monk O'Neill. I, Monk O'Neill, being crisp of wit and hale of health, do hereby bequeath all my lands and property, goods and chattels, to the Aboriginal peoples of Australia. In the advent of extinction of the Aboriginal at the time of my decease, I would then bequeath my estate to the populous Oriental nations of the north… I am very favourably disposed towards the Chinaman. On no account must my domain fall into the clutches of the predatory and upstart albino. I believe that the tides of history will swamp and wash aside this small pink tribe of mistletoe men, like insects. [*With pencil*] Change insects to dead leaves. As a coda and codicil I would like to add that I deeply regret the felling of this hillock's one tall tree, and to redress this wrong I daily nurture and fertilise with my own nitrogenous waste a feeble but promising sapling in the hope that this scion will one day attain the grandeur of its pristine sire. It is my sincere and daily death-bed wish that this tree be nourished into adulthood by those that follow. Signed, Monk O'Neill, on this the… what's the date?

MONK *walks across to the hut. Pause. He chuckles. Pause. He re-appears.*

It's my birthday. Precise to the night. This calls for a wake.

He goes across to the table, dates the will, folds it, then returns it to the eye socket. He takes the skull across to Mort's grave and puts it down.

Here's some company for you, Mort.

MONK *is on all fours and talks to the skull.*

Cheer up, Agnes. Be glad that it's all over.

He crawls off, towards the table.

Hello, ants. Enjoying the thaw? Gallop, gallop... all muscle and instinct. Come and join me at the table, friends... permit me to toss you a crumb or two.

He climbs up on to the chair, is seized by a coughing fit which climaxes in expectoration. He spits on the ground, and inspects where the sputum landed.

Sorry, Abdul.

Pause. He picks up the clock and looks at the dial. He suddenly looks up at the sky.

Well, well... the sun has broken through. A nice gesture.

He climbs up on the chair and looks at the thermometer.

Back to zero.

He gets down, pleased.

The elements have come good. This augurs well for the ensuing festivities. Now... who to invite? Mort's already arrived. Good evening, Mort. Who else?

Pause.

No one, really.

Pause.

Not a soul.

Pause.

There was a time once, even twice, when this would not have been so... oh no, they all came then... in numbers too numerous to enumerate, or remember, or forget... all gifted people, forgotten their names... however, what's in a name? I ask you, said Morrie Bund on his death bed.

Pause.

Nothing.

Pause.

That's what he said.

Pause.

Nothing.

Pause.

Pity, he was of an expansive disposition... seven inches on the slack... three erect. [*Pause. Piously*] Lovely little wife.

Pause. He walks to the grave.

I used to escort her to the cemetery every Sunday... she would kneel at the foot of Morrie's grave... a simple mound, not unlike Mort's... they're all similar, bereft of ornament... She would weep copiously, and fill a cut-glass vase with an Iceland poppy or two...

Pause.

This cannot go on, I said, from behind... a hand upon each morose shoulder...

I am inconsolable.

I understand, Dolores, but—

She caressed me lightly upon the knuckles, then loosened the buttons of her black blouse...

Pause. MONK *stares at the grave.*

We asked forgiveness of Morrie for that sin of sins... a man should be allowed to decompose in peace.

Pause.

I don't know what came over me, she sobbed.

I do.

Me.

Pause.

I hate you.

Hypocrite! I screamed... and forced her off the grave of my one true friend.

MONK *stands on the grave, defending it. Pause. He moves slowly away from the grave.*

I myself have taken the liberty of excavating for myself a grave... over there... on the slope... looking east. The traditional six feet with smooth walls of baked red clay and an inner-spring of silk on the floor. Yes. I shall crawl, on my last legs, to its edge, cast a fleeting but longing look over the pastures, then tumble in... fall onto the mattress, not quite dead... I shall lay there a while, breathing my last, listening to the corpuscles choke, ruminate on life and gaze up at the lowering sky, for it shall be evening, and discern that lurid neon... the Southern Cross, laugh a little... blaspheme the icon of it all... and feel the clay cave in... croak.

Pause. He stands.

Well, where to celebrate? I could do with a snack. Al fresco, I think... the best of everything. I shall not stint on the trough tonight.

He dashes into the hut, keen. Pause. He puts his head out.

Ovens, my chief chef, now fired, regrets to report that things are parlous in the fodder department.

MONK *disappears. Assorted noises issue from the hut as he fossicks and busies himself. He appears, attired in a tuxedo, white shirt and bow tie, with a smart hat and sunglasses. He still wears the long underwear and sandshoes.*

Nil desperandum Teucro, duce et auspice Teucro. [*Pause.*] Homer.

He walks across to the grave and sheep's skull.

Thought I might elevate the tone of the evening. What do you think, Mort?

Pause.

Silence gives consent.

Pause.

You're a tower of strength to me, Mort. Two minutes of silence for Mort, a man who was once the life of the party, who always did the right thing, a digger who has ceased to shovel, an Einstein of the stab pass and brindle chuck, a knuckler of pansies who always wore the pants, old silver-tongue, a man's man, the first off Gallipoli, one of nature's policemen. Mate.

MONK *takes off his hat, holds it over his heart and bows his head. Pause. He walks off into the hut. Pause. He re-appears carrying a home-made pie on a plate, a bottle of beer, and a glass. He has his hat on. He sits down, thinks, looking at the plate on the table, etc.*

It lacks something.

Pause. MONK *realises, and dashes off to the hut. He appears with a canvas water-bag, goes to the table, unscrews the top, and pours tomato sauce on the pie.*

[*As a waiter*] There we are, monsieur, zee pie must, ah, ow you zay, freestyle in zee sauce. [*He sits.*] Piss off, Frog. This is one area of the cuisine in which you are maladroit. Not your oval, sport.

He eats the pie.

Eat, eat, pig, pig.

He pours himself a glass of beer. He drinks the glass in one gulp.

A fine example of the brewed article.

He finishes off the pie. Pause.

An excellent pie. Worthy of the occasion.

He pours another glass, has a mouthful, sits back, and reflects.

Yes, I would like to expire this evening.

Pause.

Just look at that sunset! The clouds have parted to reveal one of nature's most banal sights.

Pause.

Drink myself into a coma.

He drinks. He sings 'Happy Birthday' to himself. Pause. He raises a full glass aloft.

Many happy returns of the day.

Pause.

To your health, Lazo.

MONK *drinks. He spills some beer on the ground.*

Sorry, ants. I am not at all vindictive by nature.

He brushes off some crumbs of pie crust from the plate onto the ground.

Into it, chaps.

He fills up his glass, takes it across to the grave, gives the sheep's skull a kick, and sets the glass down.

A last glass, Mort.

Pause.

Brrrr.

Pause.

The sun has set.

He gets up, stiffly and in pain. He walks across to the table.

Time to lower the shade.

He lowers the shade. He walks across to the drum.

Jesus, the stiffness has made a comeback.

He urinates into the drum. Pause. He peers into the drum.

Not bad for a terminal case.

He can't straighten up, so he crawls to the table, reaches up and grabs the bottle of beer which he drains. He tosses the empty bottle aside. He belches. He crawls, with difficulty, to the hut, pauses at the door and looks up.

I must remember to lower the height of this portal.

MONK *enters the hut on all fours. Silence.*

THE END

www.ingramcontent.com/pod-product-compliance
Lightning Source LLC
Chambersburg PA
CBHW040307170426
43194CB00022B/2924